Copyright 2011   David Alan Johnson

ISBN: 978-0-9843752-3-3

Sigint Press
403 Keenland Dr.
Georgetown, TX 78626

Get a Job

From the Inside Out

How to Become the Employee

Every Manager Wants to Hire

D. Alan Johnson

Copyright 2011

Table of Contents

Introduction

Conclusion

Introduction

You are looking for a Job. A real Job.

A good paying Job.

A Job with a future.

So you diligently send out resumes to many of the vacancies listed on the internet jobs board. But you aren't getting the responses you deserve. You complain bitterly to your spouse how you don't get any respect in your industry. You have years of experience, but all the big corporations are hiring these college pukes for less than half of what you are worth. Bitterness bubbles up in your throat.

I've been there. I know the feeling. And from my experience, I am here to tell you that if you continue, you are going down a road that leads to permanent under-employment. You will end up a couple of years behind your peers, and you will never be able to overcome that two or three year gap of unemployment.

I want to show you a different road, a road to self discovery. On this road, you'll learn to focus your desires and find that perfect job. And in the process you'll become the employee that companies seek out and even get in bidding wars for.

As I am writing this book, it's January 2011, and all we hear about is how bad the economy is. And yet there are people out there making fortunes in today's hard times. Corporate managers are earning $250,000 a year plus large bonuses. What's up with that?

What should we do about these people? Some politicos claim the best action is to tax the productive people and give the money to the poor and unemployed.

Does that help you, the man or woman looking for work? Well for a few minutes. But what does it do to your spirit? What happens to the individual and national work ethic? And does it not grow a sense of entitlement among the receivers? Free money is like drugs: Addicting, counterproductive, and bad for your health.

A couple of years ago I was visiting a large metropolitan church, and I asked this one man what he did for a living.

"I wait for the check," he said. I shook my head, not understanding.

"I wait for the check. Me and my family have been unemployed for about fifteen years." Fifteen years! This man has lost all hope of working. He lives a hollow life, even though he has a modest home, attends church, owns a car and a nice TV. His work is chasing one government program after another to get "free" money. But that money is not free. It comes at a terrible cost: the loss of his pride, his self worth, and his real happiness.

All the holy writings tell us that work is a gift from God. Work gives a person a sense of worth and purpose. And when our society takes that gift from someone, it's a tragedy. We take that person's abilities out of the economy, we burden the producers to care for him, but worst of all, we steal his self worth, a huge piece of the pleasure of life.

The big lie has misled us into thinking that the only ones who are making money today are those who have figured out how to oppress others and steal their money. But that is not the truth. While there are a few outlaws out there, most of those who are prospering financially are doing so because they serve other people. By building a better product, providing entertainment, or fixing your plumbing, the folks making big money are giving good things to society.

Bill Gates, the richest man in America, made his money giving us a usable personal computer and the suite of software that individuals and businesses use every second. This book is written on one of his most used software products. He has made billions of lives easier and more productive.

It's the same with the guys from Google, Steve Jobs with Apple, and Will Smith and his movies. All these folks provide society with something useful or entertaining.

You too can become like the people I've used as examples. Maybe not to the point of making millions of dollars per year, but you can work up to the level of the top five percent of earners in the world. I have done it. And I want you to know there is a way to move from a life of "waiting for the check" back to a life of self reliance and prosperity.

Stop Waiting for the Government to Create Jobs

"We need to create jobs for the people." This is a rallying cry from Washington, D.C. But the government does not create jobs. Individuals create jobs.

I can teach you to see opportunity where others only see heartache. And I can motivate you to get out into the economy and make a place for yourself. More than that, individuals can create their own job, and I'll show you how in this book.

Companies are crying out for good people. They can't find enough competent workers. That is why the guys who live out on the golf course are earning over a quarter million dollars a year. There are not enough individuals who have the combination of skills, reliability, confidence, and work ethic that companies are willing to pay big dollars for.

Go to any convention and talk to top management. They complain about the fierce competition for quality people. Their corporations have multiple high level positions open because they can't fill critical slots with just anyone. Better to have the seat vacant than fill it with a person who will cause problems.

There is a set of secrets to becoming the person whom the headhunters call. And it doesn't come down to education. Although education is important, it isn't everything. It isn't even the most important thing. There are plenty of men and women with Master's degrees and PhD's pulling the night shift at the convenience store down on the interstate.

I have wanted to write this book for a long time because I've been unemployed. I have been depressed. I've been at my wits end, with creditors calling and knocking on my door. I know that quiet panic that hovers over your head as you hide from your wife because you don't have any money to give her for groceries.

Like many of you reading this book, I have been hopeless, embarrassed, and almost in hiding from my friends and relatives. But I want you to get this message:

There is hope.

There is a way out.

Above every dreary cloud, the sun is shining.

Read on, I have something for you.

With the help of my friends I've found the secret to constant employment. In the following pages, I will roll out that secret, piece by piece. Exercise by exercise.

You Must Do the Exercises.

There will be Exercises and Action Plans to develop you into an asset that will have companies competing to hire you. Do the exercises. Complete the Action Steps and you will be amazed at the results.

I will give you some real ways to bust out of the murkiness and dependency of unemployment. There will be concrete steps, not just filmy wishes and mind games.

Read **The Secret** if you'd like. I think it's a powerful book. But instead of telling you to think like a chef, I'll give you the pots, the ingredients, and the recipe, and then I'll point you to the stove!

Chapter One: Getting Back Your Mojo

I believe that the **Lack of Self Confidence** is the greatest hindrance to employment.

Companies want to hire confident people. I am a professional pilot by trade, and I know from over thirty years of experience that aircraft owners look for pilots who have abundant self confidence. While you are standing in their office, the airplane owners can't grade your flying ability, but they can tell what **you** think of your ability. And this is usually a good indicator. A person can, if he thinks he can.

It is the same in every other industry. Whether a company is hiring a truck driver, a factory worker, a division vice president, or a traveling salesman, they are looking for someone who stands up straight, has a glint in his eye, and exudes that aura of "I can do it."

But how does one obtain or regain that confidence?

Everyone says that you "just need to get a better attitude", as if you can go out in your front yard and pick one up. Lots of companies hire motivational speakers to come in and lead their people in cheers, and then give a rousing talk titled **Altitude is Determined by Attitude**. This is great for people who are doing well and just need a little poke to get them started again.

When I was unemployed my friends would come over and give me those attitude speeches. "Buck up," they used to tell me. "Just get out there and believe you can do it." But they didn't realize how low I had sunk. Until you are down, you don't know how hard it is to get a good attitude.

My theory is different. I believe that attitude improves as you begin to act, and then spirals up as you have a series of small successes. And this leads to large successes.

Let me tell you my story.

I owned a business that failed, but due to my experience in the industry, I was immediately hired as the general manager by a former competitor. After six months I was fired, as I deserved to be. A big lesson for me, by the way: Work in an area where you possess strengths. Management is not my strength.

For the next six weeks, I scoured the want ads and sent out resumes. I got a couple of interviews, but no offers. I know now why those businessmen didn't offer me a job: I looked like I was beaten. That's how I felt and it showed.

I descended into depression. Not wanting to leave my room, I spent all day playing solitaire. This went on for about two months as our cash reserves dwindled.

One sunny morning in December, I got a big wake up call. I heard a loud knock on my door, and when I opened it, there stood a representative from my lender wanting to repossess my car. I invited him in and begged for a two week extension. Because I had always paid on time before, he agreed.

I went out in my garage, took inventory of my stuff, and put an ad in the paper. (This was long before Craig's List.) Within a week I sold off my tools, the old pickup I was restoring, a spare engine, ladders, a canoe, and my bicycle. You can't believe how much straighter I stood when I walked up to my wife and gave her money for the back car payments and groceries.

This was my first success. My confidence increased and my attitude improved.

Next I called my friends and asked if they knew of any jobs. (Make a note. This is called networking and we will cover it in the following chapters.) During the weeks before, I had been too embarrassed to call them and let them know of my plight. After the fourth call, a friend told me that, while his company had no openings, they were having problems getting some work done.

His large communication company was bidding out some construction work that no one else wanted since the project was so small. The job entailed digging a series of holes to measure the depth of several fiber optic cables. A big road building project was coming through, and the cable company needed to be sure how deep their fiber optic cables were buried so there would be no accidental breaks. They needed twelve holes dug to physically measure the depth of the cables. I got the information and put together a bid.

Calling another friend, I told him I needed the best backhoe operator he knew. I couldn't afford to break a fiber optic cable! He gave me some names of good operators he had used in the pipeline business.

Two days later I had a breakfast meeting with this one old guy, and he told me that he charged out his backhoe at $250 for a half day. He was more expensive than any other operator I talked with, but I figured he was worth it. Besides, he had an insurance policy that would meet the criteria for the contract.

I bid $865.00 per hole and won the bid, since I was the only bidder. Specified in my bid was that each hole was to be paid in advance.

We dug that first hole on a cold morning in late January. First, using an electronic wand, the company technician located the cable and placed flags in the ground in a row, marking the route of the cable. My backhoe guy then dug a trench parallel and offset to the right side. Now the tech and I got down in the hole, and he used his wand to locate the cable along the wall of the trench. I dug sideways with a short shovel until we uncovered the cable. The tech took the measurement from the surface, took photos, and we covered up the hole. Done by ten o'clock.

After paying the backhoe operator, and counting my gas and the donuts I brought, I cleared $600 that morning. We did two holes a week for the next six weeks.

That's how I got into the construction business. For the next year and a half, I ran a one man show. I put an ad in the paper that I did remodels and small projects. My only assets were my car and my business cards.

People would call me complaining they couldn't get anyone to bid on their projects because the jobs were too small or too complicated. I would call a subcontractor suitable for the job: Bricklayer, tile guy, trim and cabinets, whatever I needed. I got the names from a friend at church who owned a big construction company.

The owner would show me the job and I would make sketches. I would come back later with the subcontractor in tow. We would inspect the job location, and I would get a firm bid from the sub.

For example, I'll tell you about one of our jobs. A man wanted an eight-foot tall cinderblock wall built around his backyard. These were very popular in South Texas for a few years. I brought in the best wall guy in the county.

After the mason measured the length and checked the soil, he bid $4,000 to build the wall. Knowing that my father's friend had just paid over ten thousand for a similar wall, I went to the owner later that day. I showed up with a drawing, a nice written proposal, and a contract.

"With a yard as big as yours, and adding two gates, I need to get $8,200," I said. The guy squeezed his chin.

"I don't see any paint in this bid. I'll need the wall painted."

"Okay. I'll redo my bid then."

"I'll tell you what, you throw in the paint, and it's a deal," the property owner said with a little smile.

"Alright. Paint is included." I wrote on the bid and inserted into the contract that I'd throw in the paint, his choice of color. We both initialed the changes. He signed the contract.

"That will be $4,000 down payment." The down payment was spelled out in the contract. The property owner handed me a personal check, and I had the money to pay the subcontractor the $2,000 he needed to start. Plus I had some money for mama.

We finished the wall two weeks later, and my wife and I, along with my two young daughters painted the inside and outside of the wall, two coats. My profit: $3,840.

Believe me, this series of victories was a huge shot to my confidence, and led to me getting hired again as a pilot. Not just as any pilot, but as a military contractor as I had been years ago. I got the job I had dreamed about. Now I work 28 days on, and 21 days off while earning well above $150,000.

Most people don't realize that you can't land a great job until you can inspire your prospective employers. You must have the confidence that will create trust in the manager who is hiring. And just like you can't climb the mountain until you get past the foothills, I am going to give you a blueprint to gain that confidence.

When you go to interview, you must know who you are and what you possess. You must have some wins in your column, some cards up your sleeve, and some tools in your toolbox. I am not talking about tricks. I'm talking about being so prepared and understanding yourself so well that you inspire massive trust in the heart of your employer.

The greater the trust you inspire, the higher the position you will be offered, and the greater the pay and perks you will be able to demand.

Chapter Two: What Are Your Assets?

You will never convince your prospective employer of your abilities until you convince yourself. In this section, we will embark on a journey together. Along the way, you will see some sights. Then you will do the first of your exercises.

Where are you now?

The first step in any navigation problem is finding out where you are. We are going to navigate to that perfect job. The one you've always dreamed of. But first we have to know our true whereabouts. I'm not talking about geographical coordinates. I am talking about your abilities, your character, and your mental state.

Sometimes it's hard to look at ourselves. Not with our eyes, mind you. But with that inner discernment that will tell you who and what you really are.

Often, the "man in the mirror" is our worst critic. He knows our weaknesses and our failures. We meet him every morning and he can be like the devil, telling you lies.

"Who are you to be wanting a high paying job?"

You must convince that man in the mirror that you are a confident and worthy individual. Until you convince him, you won't convince others.

Take Inventory

When any good businessman needs a snapshot of his business, he takes inventory. After I got fired from my management job, my vision narrowed, and I lost sight of my assets. All I could think about was how I had been wronged. (After a couple of years of thinking it over, I know why I got fired, and I learned that hard lesson.)

But I focused on the wrong thing for months. I want you to learn from my mistakes. You must be able to view and then augment your assets. And these assets are what you will use to make a future and a fortune for you and your family.

In descending order of importance, these are your assets:

- **Your character**
- **Your intangible assets**
- **Your tangible assets**

Remember these three categories. Your future employer will look deeply into each of these areas when he decides to hire you or pass you over. He might not even realize that he goes through this process.

Stick with me and I'll explain how and why the hirer values each asset group. Understanding his motivations and desires for an employee is vital to landing that big job.

Tangible Assets

Since these are the easiest to see and count, we'll talk about them first. Tangible means something that you can see and touch. Tangible Assets include:

- Physical Appearance
- Age
- Licenses and Certifications
- Your House
- Your Car
- Your Cash
- Your Possessions such as Clothes and Toys.

When talking to some of my unemployed friends, they often make excuses for not going after a good job. And these excuses show that they don't understand the relative value of their assets, and they don't understand the hiring process.

Some of the excuses that I hear all the time are:

- "I don't have the money to get a nice new suit."
- "I can't show up for an interview in my old car."
- "I'm too old/young."
- "I can't even afford to have a decent resume written."

These people are looking at the wrong assets. I know people who are in the 70's and hired for important positions. One man I met last September told me that he was 75 years old and wanted to retire, but companies kept hiring him as a consultant to oversee the manufacturing process on valves used in nuclear power plants.

"Why don't you just retire?" I asked him.

"They keep offering me too much money," he complained.

On the other end of the age scale, a friend of mine, Richard W. was hired right out of college for an executive intelligence position in a Fortune 500 company.

A decent suit and a professional looking resume are good things to have, but they are not critical or even that important.

The **Number One** excuse that I hear most often is:

"You have to have money to make money."

That is a FALSE statement. Believe me, the first two sets of assets, your character and your intangible assets are so, so much more important than your physical assets.

In the 1930's Henry Ford, the founder of Ford Motor Company was considered by most to be the richest man in the world. But many don't know that Mr. Ford went bankrupt before restarting his company when he was in his forties, and then he became wildly successful.

The story is told about a reporter who knew of Mr. Ford's bankruptcy twenty years before. In an interview he asked Mr. Ford:

"What if you go bankrupt again? Aren't you afraid of losing all your money in this Depression?"

"No, son, I'm not afraid," Ford said. "Take away everything I have, and I'll be a millionaire again in a year."

You see, Henry Ford understood one of the truths of the universe:

Tangible assets come from intangible assets.

Character, friendships, honesty, hard work, reliability, knowledge, confidence, and perseverance bring riches. Not the other way around.

Today's news is filled with stories of people who have won the lottery. Twenty-five million dollars is put into their account in one day. But does this money change that person into a wise, generous, hardworking, reliable person with lots of connections to other people? No.

And a few months later we hear that these same people, rich as a sultan last year, are bankrupt now. Without those intangible assets, money will not remain. Foolishness repels riches.

When one takes inventory, one must understand his assets and the relative values of those assets. So, let's get to know our two most valuable assets.

Character

Character is who you are. It is the measure of your inner man. And people judge your character by your outward "characteristics". In this book I argue that a person can change his character.

How? How do you change character? By changing your characteristics. Change your actions for a few days and you will change your habits. Continue your habits for a few weeks and you will change your character.

Don't listen to those defeatists who will tell you that you can't change yourself.

"That's just the way you are," they will say. Don't listen to them. Instead look to your heroes and see how they grew and changed during their lives.

You can change your character by changing one action at a time, by working hard at being a better person, by becoming more aware of yourself and others.

There are people of good character and people of bad character applying for the same position. What type of character will an employer look for? That is an easy answer:

He looks for a person of good character filled with at least most of the following characteristics.

- Honesty
- A Good Work Ethic
- Wisdom
- Thankfulness
- Perseverance
- Generosity
- Kindness
- Reliability

I have been a hiring manager and I know several. Plus, I having been a private military contractor for 25 years, I've changed contracts (jobs) every two years or so. I tell you this so you will believe me when I say that hirers look deeply into your character.

Most hiring managers don't even know that they do so. But when they call your references they don't ask how good a technician you are, but what kind of person you are. How are you to work with?

In this book, I lay out a small exercise to build your character. But you must be the builder and finisher of your character. Your spouse can help you. Start today by sending "Thank you" notes to those who have helped you.

Do something for someone who will never be able to repay you. Every day build your character by doing one small good deed.

As you develop character, you will begin to see the value of the next section.

Intangible Assets

You read any great work of philosophy or spirituality and it will tell you that your success comes from "intangible assets". Intangible means unable to be touched or seen. Outward success comes from the inside. Or as one writer said, "You must have hundreds of private victories before you enjoy a public victory."

How do we develop those intangibles? Other books tell you to change your thinking:

- "Don't worry. Be happy."
- "Think positive."
- "Feel good about yourself."

They promise that if you change your thinking to the positive, you will change your outward success. Just have the right feelings and good things will come to you.

I argue that those commands are impossible to accomplish. They are not doable because feelings are derived from actions. Actions are not derived from feelings.

You Develop Intangible Assets through Effort

The farmer cannot "think" grain into his barn with happy thoughts. He must get a piece of land. He must plow, sow, tend the field, and then harvest the crop. Then will he have grain in his silo. Then he will be happy. And then he will think positive thoughts and feel good about himself.

Just so, it is the same with your happiness, positive thinking, and feeling of self confidence. You must act first, and these attitudes and feelings will follow.

All successful men of action, if they are truthful, tell of passing through periods of setbacks, doubt, depression, and despair. Read any of the great men's autobiographies. The first thing many of them had to overcome was their own self doubt.

But they didn't give up or give in to those doubts and depressions. Julius Caesar, Napoleon, Lincoln, and Churchill all had terrible reversals in their lives. Yet they never gave up. Likewise, only by pushing on by force of will, by perseverance, and with the correct actions, will you arrive at success and have those good feelings.

In his books, Anthony Robbins talks of finding the right goal and then "taking massive action" to reach that goal. You see, we must first work before we enjoy the reward.

In our mission to enhance our hire-ability, we need to also take inventory of our intangible assets. Believe me, employers look very hard at these intangibles, even though some of them don't realize it.

While this is not an exhaustive list, these are some of the intangible assets:

- Good Health

- Enthusiasm
- Network of Contacts
- Specialized Training/Skills
- Education
- Ability to Persuade
- Social Graces
- Experience
- Creativity
- Leadership

The Man in the Mirror

Let's start our inventory. Once again, we are going to have a heart to heart talk with the man in the mirror. Get up and go to the mirror. Stare at that man or woman who looks back at you. Does that person possess the character traits that will bring happiness, confidence, and fulfilling employment?

We will often return to meet with the man in the mirror. I guarantee that if you persevere and perform the exercises to follow, you will enjoy seeing the man in the mirror. You will meet him with a smile, because you will become happy with who you are.

Work Ethic

Let's begin building our character by starting with work ethic. Do you have a good work ethic? Of course, you answer, "Yes." But your work ethic is not just for work at your job. You see, you must already "be" a hard worker before you go to the interview. And only by being a hard worker already can you answer that inevitable interview question:

"How would you rate your work ethic?"

A good interviewer will know in an instant what your work ethic is like by your reaction. And the only way you will have the response he is looking for is to already believe that you are a worker. You will only believe that when you have proven it to yourself though regular hard work.

An employer won't take a risk that you will "become" a hard worker after he hires you.

One thing about working hard: You never know who is watching you.

Success Story Number One

One morning I was sitting in the donut shop in Smithville, Texas enjoying a maple frosted donut.

An Asian man about thirty years old walked into the shop and greeted the Cambodian woman behind the counter in some Asian language. He walked over to my table.

"Are you enjoying your donut, sir?" he asked me in good English.

"Yes, I am."

"I am so glad. You see, I own this donut shop," the young man said with pride. "May I sit with you?"

"Of course." I motioned to the bench on the other side of my booth.

"I came to the United States five years ago as a political refugee from Cambodia. When I got here, I could speak no English and I had no money.

"But I got a job in a bakery in Los Angeles washing dishes and cleaning up. During the two years I worked there, I learned English." He smiled and motioned to the girl and she brought her boss a cup of coffee.

"One day, one of the flour salesmen asked me to go to lunch with him, so I went. At lunch the salesman said:

> 'We've been watching you for the last two years. You are a hard worker. Your boss says you're never late or sick, and you treat his business like it's yours. How would you like to have your own donut shop?'

> 'But I have no money to start a shop. I have no credit. And I don't know how to run a donut shop,' I said.

> 'That's not important. Our company wants to expand into Central Texas. We'll find you a location, loan you the money, and teach you everything you need to know. We have

a complete business blueprint. We have everything except someone who will work hard at the bakery business.'

'Why would you do this for me?'

'Oh, there's a catch. We're in the business of selling bakery supplies. You'll have to sign a contract that you'll buy all your sugar, flour, coffee, cups, napkins, and advertising through our company for the next ten years.'

The young man sat back and sipped his coffee, waiting for my reply.

"So this is the donut shop you started," I said.

"Oh no. I started that first one in Dallas. I now own thirteen donut shops and I'm a millionaire. This is the only country in the world where a man with nothing— nothing— can become a millionaire in five years. Thank you for coming to my donut shop. Enjoy."

With that the young man got up and left. I sat thinking about his story for a long time.

Today you can drive around Central Texas from the little town of George West north to Amarillo and find what we call the Asian Donut shops. Most of them are called "Donut Palace", "Super Donuts", or "Happy Donuts". They are often in old buildings that were once gasoline stations. And when you enjoy one of their excellent pastries, remember the man who got there by hard work.

Lots of folks will discount that story, saying that things like that never happen. But I know they do. My father started his supermarket in a similar fashion, getting financing and business advice from a grocery wholesaler in return for signing a long term agreement to purchase his groceries and supplies through them.

Others of you will say, "That donut guy was just lucky." I guess you could say that.

I remember when I was a young pilot, telling a millionaire business owner that he was lucky. His reply stuck in my brain for these thirty years:

"Yes son, I am lucky."

"The harder I work, the luckier I get."

You see, there is always work to do. You might not get paid today for your work, but it will pay off. People notice your shined shoes and clean car. Your study and preparation will vault you above other applicants for that dream job.

I'll show you how to work at building your network and getting contacts to get you inside to see the hiring manager at your target company. Work hard especially when you aren't being paid.

Exercise Number One: Demonstrate Your Work Ethic

For some of you, this will be the easiest exercise. For others, it will be tough. I want you to find some work to do today. Mow your grass, rake leaves, clean out your garage, and/or wash and vacuum your car.

Work is noble. And you must convince yourself that you are a hard worker.

Is it easy? No.

Is it right? Yes.

At one time I worked in the corporate intelligence department of a multinational oil company, and one of the things they checked before hiring any executive was the look of his house and car. They would send someone to drive down his street and check out his personal habits. A clean car, a well trimmed yard, and a maintained house were minimums. If the prospect failed here, he never got another interview.

We find it too easy to spend the days watching movies or surfing the internet. Change a bit of your character. Become a person of action.

Find a piece of work to do right now.

You live in an apartment and there is no work like this? Then find a park where you can pick up trash. Find an alley or a stream clogged with garbage and clean it up. Come on. No excuses.

Work will improve your sense of well being, get you moving toward some physical activity, and best of all, you will convince yourself that you are a hard worker.

Remember, you never know who is watching.

Chapter Three: Developing Wisdom

We've already talked about boosting your work ethic. By the way, have you done the first exercise? If you haven't, please do it now. This manual will be of little use to you if you do not perform the exercises.

Wisdom

What is wisdom? And what does it have to do with getting a good job?

Wisdom is the ability to make sensible decisions based upon knowledge. Therefore, the shallowest motive for gaining wisdom is to become a business asset. CEOs of large corporations pay huge money to advisors who can look through reams of information and recommend a wise course of action.

The wise man can see how actions taken today will play out in the future. He understands cause and effect. Not that he is a fortune teller. But the wise can see that one course will lead to success and another to failure.

I hope you will make the pursuit of wisdom a lifelong activity. Some of the fallout from that pursuit will be a happier family, a peaceful and useful life, and the respect of other people of wisdom.

Foolishness is the opposite of wisdom, yet we often embrace foolishness because it is so much easier. In the above example, after I was fired from my General Manager position, I was hurt. I just wanted to retreat to my cave and recover. A natural response. But was it wise? No, it was foolish.

If I had been wise, I would have seen that without massive action, our family money would soon be gone. It should have come as no surprise that the bank would want to repossess my Suburban. I hadn't returned their phone calls or made a payment in three months.

The wise man does what is right even when it is hard.

I remember being a young boy in the little town of Jenks, Oklahoma. My grandfather and I were walking across an old gravel parking lot just after the rain. Thinking how smart I was, I went ahead of him, and looking down I avoided all the puddles. But soon I found myself over a hundred yards away from Grandpa's truck and on the wrong side of the parking lot.

"Stay there, Son. I'll drive over to you," the old man called out with a laugh in his voice.

When I got into the truck, my grandfather used the next few minutes to show me the lesson of the parking lot. You see, as a wise man, he recognized an opportunity to teach his grandson an important truth.

"Son, life is just like that parking lot. You have to look up to know where you're going. Avoid the puddles if you can. But sometimes you've got to go through a puddle to get to the truck. Set your eye on where you want to go, and then don't let anything stop you."

I was six years old.

The foolish man avoids the puddles in life, always taking the easier path. But to get to your goal, you have to walk through a few puddles, you sometimes have to swim across a river, and occasionally you'll have to climb the mountain.

Talking about the world of employment, the foolish man will sit and collect his unemployment compensation for two years or more, hoping that he'll find a job. You see, he is taking the easy way, avoiding all the puddles. On the other hand, the wise man will say to his family, "This area is dying. We need to move to where there is more opportunity."

Or he will see that his type of work has been made obsolete. He might have been one of the best Video Cassette Recorder (VCR) engineers in the nation. But that is now an obsolete technology. The wise man understands that he must retrain and move on with the times.

People have been moving to better places for thousands of years. They fled famines, political persecution, droughts, and poverty. Our forefathers risked death to come to the new world. Our grandparents escaped the dustbowl to found cities and factories. And our parents moved for good jobs so that we could go to college.

Or the foolish man will say, "I can get more money collecting unemployment than by working." He does not regard consequences of this "easy money": the lost business contacts he could have made, the work experience he would have gained. Worst of all is the way that prospective employers view his actions. People collecting unemployment are seen as the least desirable applicants for an open job.

Wise men see the long view.

Social and Economic Strata

Another item that the wise man understands is his position in life. Don't misunderstand me. I am not saying that a person is frozen in a certain social strata. No, I am saying that the wise man understands in which strata he lives right now and where he wants to go.

How can you move up unless you understand where you are now? How can you change if you don't know what to do differently?

American social strata are not fixed as in some societies. Men and women can move freely between these social and economic levels. Think of the different parts of society as social and economic tribes. These tribes are marked by varying education levels, income levels, different attitudes, language, clothing, and actions. Some tribes regularly make five times the money of the other tribes while working much less. Observe these differences and compare yourself to the people you want to be like.

Now make a plan to change what you need to change so that you can move up into another tribe. Some of the obvious items are clothing and grooming. You might enjoy your long hair and beard, the leather motorcycle vest, jeans, and boots. But none of these will prepare you to join the tribe of the Employed.

The tribe called the Employed watch their language. While it has become popular to curse, even for women, the Employed refrain. When was the last time you heard top management or a business owner curse or make crude comments? Of course there are always exceptions, but the norm among the Employed is that they express themselves without dropping down to cursing. Changing the habit of using the F-bomb can be difficult. But you can do it. Practice.

Exercise Number Two

Cut your hair, shave your face, and buy a suit. You don't need a $40 haircut. My wife cut my hair for years. And you don't need a $1,000 suit. Check out the consignment shops and the Good Will Store. My brother-in-law regularly finds like-new clothes for a couple of dollars an item.

I know this doesn't sound like it belongs in the section on wisdom. But it does. The wise owl camouflages himself so that he appears as the stump of a limb. You also must fit into the surroundings where you will be hanging out, and look like the people who will be hiring you or you make it many times harder for yourself. Save your old clothes for when you go the biker bars on the weekend.

One other thing you must have is a business card. You can get free business cards from VistaPrint.com. Design a simple, clean card with your name, profession, and contact information. Don't put too much on the card. Remember, "Less is More."

Mine says D. Alan Johnson, Author, and then my website and my email. This is important. Don't skip this one.

D. Alan Johnson
Author

www.dalanjohnson.com
driver601@gmail.com

Physical Fitness

One of the great secrets of employment is that employers hire fit people. I'm not necessarily talking about the "gym rats" that have all those huge muscles. Many hirers find them a bit over the top.

But, one cannot deny that a person who is normal weight with a healthy glow to their skin will get more opportunities than a person thirty or more pounds overweight. I know you want to complain, and tell me that it isn't fair. You can provide research that shows overweight people can do just as good a job as a slender person.

I am not arguing that. However, I am saying that if you want to get a good job, your chances of getting hired go up by a factor of four or five if you are slender compared to showing up at the interview thirty or more pounds overweight.

This is one of those points in your life that is a "Time for Truth." If you are overweight or under strength, now is the time to do something about it. No excuses. You are talking with someone who has been thirty pounds overweight and severely out of shape.

In 1996, after a couple of years of owning my own business, I had gotten fat and lazy. A new contract opened up and I was recalled as a pilot. As I got off the airliner and walked across the ramp at Cabinda, Angola, my new boss greeted me with, "Well if it isn't the Pillsbury Dough Boy."

I knew right then I had to do something and do it right away. The next morning I found out that our staff meetings were held during the boss's daily three mile walk. I had a hard time those first few days keeping up. I was so out of breath that I couldn't even speak when asked a question.

But I started working out: A few pushups, a solo walk in the evening, and then regular trips to our "Flintstone Gym".

The war with Dr. Joseph Savimbi in Angola was winding down and so my boss took the opportunity to build a gym. He used drive chain off a destroyed Soviet tank and some pipe to build a lat pull down machine. We hung flywheels off of the ends of a tail rotor drive shaft from a downed helicopter for our bench press bar. Piston pins from the tank engine made good hand weights.

Within four months, not only had I lost over thirty pounds, but I had transformed my body from flab to muscle. All my clothes fit better, my face was no longer bloated, and I could walk the three miles without even starting to breathe hard.

If I, as a middle aged man, could do this, anyone can. All it takes is the discipline to apply a little effort on a regular basis. Go for a walk every day, use the stairs instead of the elevator, push your plate away while there is still some food on it, and you will see changes in your body.

I know that not everyone can afford to go to a gym, but you don't need it. Look up exercises you can do at home, and then do them. Push-ups, deep knee bends, and pull-ups on a tree limb in my back yard help me keep my weight where I like it. It doesn't take but ten or fifteen minutes every day. But you must do enough that you get your pulse up to maximum. Check out this article and look up Dr. Al Sears. Get his newsletters about short bursts of exercise leading to a leaner you.

http://www.totalhealthbreakthroughs.com/author/dr-al-sears/

http://www.dralsearsmd.com

Wisdom is a characteristic that employers will pay huge amounts of money to obtain. If you develop wisdom and display it in your daily walk, people, including employers, will notice.

Take time to be quiet and think. Put together cause and effect of your past actions, for today you are the sum total of your decisions and actions from the past. Use what you have learned about yourself to project into the future what your actions might bring.

Read some of the Wisdom Literature that our forefathers have left for us. I like the **Book of Proverbs** by Solomon. Others read Plato, **The Prophet** or the **Book of**

Five Rings. Whatever it is, find books to read about wisdom. Remember the saying, "Leaders are Readers." No excuses. You can check these books out of the library for free.

See yourself as others see you, and then change yourself to be better, whether it be your clothes, your hair, your speech, or your weight. A wise person not only looks at others he looks at himself. He realizes that it is difficult for another to see his inner person when distracted by the outer person.

The subject of wisdom will take up the rest of your life. After you take hold of it, you will want to pass it on to your grandchildren and your valued subordinates.

Chapter Four: Deciding On Your Path

Life is a journey. Most people wander through life just like, as a little boy, I wandered around that parking lot. They avoid the puddles and don't much care where they end up as long as they don't have to put out too much effort to get there.

But you, the man seeking wisdom, will look off into the distance and decide where you want to go. You will decide on a certain path, and you will not be deterred. I think that this is more difficult today than ever before. After all, you are faced with thousands of choices. You could become a weapons designer or a wedding planner, a butcher or a banker. We must find some way to cut through all those choices and focus. Until we focus, the odds of nabbing a good job are low.

The story is told about a hunter who topped a ridge and saw a herd of elk moving slowly through the meadow.

"There are so many that I can't miss," he said. His guide pressed up close and whispered in his ear.

"No. Take aim on just one animal or you'll miss for sure."

Remember the advice of the hunting guide. If you aim at all the jobs, you will never hit one. Focus.

Many who read this book have already decided where they are going. They just need some encouragement and a few tips to continue their journey. But if you have not decided, then the next few pages are for you.

Are you answering any and all want ads that sound like good pay and not too much work? You see an ad for a forklift driver, and you apply. You see an ad for a project manager, so you shoot off a resume. Some buddy tells you they are hiring at a refinery at the port, so you ask him to put your name in.

If this sounds like you, then we need to talk.

"It doesn't matter what I do, as long as I make good money at that job," you will tell me.

But is does matter to your prospective employer. I want you to look at your resume from the hirer's point of view. You see, the wise man can see and understand another person's viewpoint and motivations.

Let's pretend that the human resources manager at a refinery is looking at your resume and the other applicant's resume side by side.

Your resume has a letter attached from your friend with a glowing personal recommendation. Your work history shows that you have worked as a truck driver for a beer company, a salesman for a copier manufacturer, and that you just got laid off from a paper mill where you were a forklift driver. Your education ends with an Associate Degree in Business from the local community college.

The other resume has a cover letter from the applicant explaining that he has always been fascinated with the refining business. Due to financial constraints he had to drop out of the university where he was majoring in chemical engineering. He states that his goal is to become a refinery plant manager in the years to come.

The only employment experience listed on his resume is that he did a summer internship at the Valero refinery in Aruba last summer.

Believe me, the hirer will interview the young man who is focused and excited about the refining business before he will call you, even though you have more education, more experience, and a great recommendation letter from your friend.

You may not realize it, but your resume is being passed over again and again for those who show that they are passionate and focused on a certain industry.

One of the reasons that bosses percolate to the top of their companies is that they love what they do. They want to hire others who also love their kind of business, because they know and understand those types of people. They believe that a focused person is a better risk and will do a better job.

These people in hiring positions believe that an unfocused person will never become the passionate, knowledgeable employee who is happy and thankful to be in their perfect job. And these happy employees are what managers want to hire.

So, let's focus.

Work in an Industry You Enjoy

Sit down and let's talk about what you want to do.

It is a great blessing to get up every day and go to a job that you love. You know what I mean. There are ship captains who can't wait to be at sea again. I've seen truck drivers get out of their big rig and look back at the truck with love in their eye. I know teachers who can't wait to get back into the classroom to impart some jewel of understanding to their children.

You can have that dream job. And, it is ironic that you will make more money in the job that you would do for free than in the job that they have to pay you big money to consider. So, let's find out what that dream job is.

Finding What You Like to Do

A rich old man once told me about his two greatest tools for making money:

- The yellow legal pad, and
- A good quality pen.

Don't discount this advice. Get yourself a yellow legal pad and a good pen. Not a free pen you picked up that has advertising on it, but one that gives you pleasure as it glides over the page. There is magic there.

I have graduated from the legal pad to a spiral bound notebook; the kind you can pick up for a dollar. Don't try to do this on a computer. There is something about the connection between the writing hand and the brain.

Now that you are properly armed, we can begin.

Write on your legal pad the activities that you like. Don't worry if they are not what you might call "business skills". Write them down.

This is what my list looks like. (And I wrote these down, just now, as fast as I could without thinking too much.)

- Flying
- Military stuff
- Intelligence (CIA)
- History
- Reading
- Writing
- Singing

I have a perfect job. You see, my day job is that I fly an ISR (Intelligence, Surveillance, Reconnaissance) aircraft as a contractor for the Department of Defense. I feel that I impact history, I have lots of time off, and while I work I get to travel (forgot to add that one). Plus, this job gives me plenty of time to write, which is my second passion.

Put down this book. Pick up your pen and write your list.

Do it now.

This is important. The first things that come to mind are usually the best and most powerful.

Write Out Your List.

Now that you have your list, look it over and find the items that inspire you. But remember, there are certain activities that by their nature do not pay well. For example, I don't know of any poets who have made a good living writing and performing poetry. My advice is that you take each of the items that you wrote down and monetize them.

Look back at my list, and you will see **Singing**. I love to sing, especially old gospel music in four-part harmony. But there's not much demand out there for a baritone specializing in gospel music.

Writing is another item that doesn't pay well.

Friends of mine have listed things like photography, scuba diving, basketball, and golf. Lots of golf. But these things won't make you any money. You can become a great golfer, and never earn any money at it. (However, golf is a great networking skill, especially when you get into upper management.) You might take a great photo, but it won't pay your mortgage.

Remember; concentrate on activities that will serve others.

On the other hand, you can become a good salesman and make a small fortune, become a good technician and be set for life, or learn to be a project manager able to shepherd projects through to completion and be in constant demand.

Check off the items on your list that could be used to persuade a company to create a position for you. On my list you see that I like intelligence. More and more businesses are using the precepts of gathering facts and analyzing them for competitive advantages. I know that I can get a job in that field. I've researched it. And should I ever lose my flight physical, or get tired of traveling so much, I just might go into that field.

I could use my love of reading and writing to generate valuable reports and business plans for senior management. With an understanding of history and the military, I would be a valuable asset to any company that operates in a conflict area.

Do you see how you can use your imagination to pour yourself into a position in a company?

Success Story Number Two

(This story is true, but it must remain vague due to the parties involved.)

A good friend of mine got out of the Army about twelve years ago. After taking inventory of his likes and abilities, he targeted a company where he wanted to work.

He drove from Maryland to Oregon and stayed in a hotel. First thing the next morning he walked into the front office of this medium sized corporation dressed in a nice suit and carrying his plan in a fine leather portfolio.

"Good morning, sir," the receptionist said. "Do you have an appointment?"

"No. I don't have an appointment. But I need to see the President, Mr. Blain (not his real name)."

"You can't see Mr. Blain without an appointment."

"I will see Mr. Blain, and he will hire me as the Director of Business Development for South America. You call him and tell him I'm here." My friend delivered this statement with a friendly confidence and a mysterious smile.

After a short silence, the receptionist called the president of the corporation, and told him about my friend.

"He'll see you now," she said, shocked that my friend could go right in.

"Sir, you have no business presence in South America, one of the fastest growing areas of the world," my friend stated as he sat down across from the president.

"I have a plan to penetrate that market." He handed the president a formal action plan based on the military plans he'd written for years. "I've worked South America for the US Army and I am friends with many military leaders and politicians. We can get lots of business down there in short order."

The president took a moment to look over the plan. The first part was the action plan which included the customers targeted, how they would be approached, and how my friend planned to close each sale.

The second part of the plan included the timeline with interim objectives and yearly sales goals.

The last page had a cash flow projection stating how much money needed to be allocated to travel and entertainment, his salary, the projected income, and my friend's commission structure and year-end bonus.

The president started negotiating with my friend. The haggling was not about whether my friend would get hired, but about how much he would be paid!

My friend got the job and made lots of money by selling this high end product all over South

America. After a few years, bored by success, he took an executive position with another company in South America.

This man convinced a major company to hire him and create a slot for him where none existed before. How did he do this?

He first researched the company and found a way to make them money. Then he convinced the president that he would deliver more to the company than what the company would pay out for his services. My friend showed that he knew how to plan and prepare, how to target decision makers, and that he could be persuasive.

My friend earned a six-figure income derived from his ability to sell himself to this major corporation.

Back to our list. My friend in the story above took his strengths and applied them to one company. You can do the same thing. Work on your list. Rewrite it a few times. Change the order. See where you can monetize each of your abilities, ranking them from the most profitable to the least. Now post that list where you can see it from your desk or kitchen table while we continue with setting your goals.

Below is a list of questions to help you focus. Write down your answers and think about why you responded the way you did. This will guide you and make your mind start thinking about what type of work you are best suited for.

Do you want to work outdoors or indoors? Explain.

Do you understand machinery? Can you explain why a submarine sinks and why an air conditioner cools? What type of machinery do you like best?

When you see two people in a disagreement, can you understand each person's point of view?

Do you like to know what will happen every day when you go to work? Or do you look forward to a new challenge or moving to a new location every few days?

Are you fascinated by the way a certain mechanism works or are you more interested in the overall system? For example, would you rather know how the diesel electric drive system works on a locomotive, or how freight moves through the rail systems from pick-up to delivery.

Get a Viewpoint from an Outside Observer

Just out of the Army, and 22 years old, I struggled with what type of career I wanted. My father suggested that I become an evangelist, and sent me to Dallas to spend a week with a preacher friend of his. When I decided against that, he suggested that I visit his doctor and find out about going into medicine. After half a day I knew that I wanted nothing to do with healthcare.

This visitation process continued through accountants, bankers, and insurance brokers. But I could never find anything that really appealed to me.

Each afternoon after interviewing one of my father's friends, I would take my beautiful wife to a levee where we had a great view of the airplanes landing at the airport. I loved watching the airplanes land as the sun set. After the second week of spending our evenings watching the aircraft, my wife asked me one of the most important questions of my life:

"Why don't you just get a job at the airport?"

From that day I researched becoming a pilot. Her question set me off in a direction that resulted in a happy a prosperous career. I don't know if I would have ever started down that road without her insight.

After you have searched your heart, written out your desires, and pondered your future, ask the advice of someone you love and respect. They may have a perspective of your talents that you lack. They may see something in you that you have missed. Listen to those who love you and know you.

That view from the outside is why there is also real value in having a job coach. Even the greatest quarterbacks have coaches. Bing Crosby, one of the finest singers who ever lived, continued to take voice lessons into his 60's. Get a coach. They can see facets of your personality, job hunting plan, and networking that you can't. With that different perspective, they can advise you and point you in a direction that you might never have considered. The money you invest in a coach will blossom, and you will be employed much faster than going on your own.

Write Articles

When I coach someone during a job search, I advise my client to write a series of articles for submission to websites like www.ezinearticles.com and www.gather.com. (You can view my articles on both these sites.) By concentrating on writing, you will delve deeply into those things you feel you need to communicate. Think about what you want to write during long walks or when you are driving on a road trip.

After ten articles, I can tell where a person's real passions lie. Typically, a person will compose his first couple of articles on subjects that he feels he "ought to" write about: His old job or his political views. But as the articles start to flow, I can see the subjects change and gravitate to the areas of his passions: Health, spirituality, history, free trade, etc.

Then I know, as a coach, some areas to explore and maybe which way to point my client.

A side benefit to writing articles is that the job hunter gets a bigger presence on the internet. You can bet your savings that any hiring manager worth a nickel will google your name to see what he can discover about you. If he sees a series of well written articles showing your passion and expertise in his field, you will jump in front of the other applicants.

Exercise Number Three

Seek out someone who can give you an outside observation of the type of job you might find enjoyable. For if you love your job, chances are you will excel. Plus you will wake up every morning excited to go to work.

The person you choose needs to be someone you respect and admire. Perhaps your father, wife, or best friend. For some of us, those relationships are filled with too much baggage. By that, I mean that they are too close to us. The next best person could be a teacher or mentor.

If you can afford it, hire a professional coach. They can interview you and not only give you a direction, but plug you into their vast network of industry insiders.

Ponder on the advice you are given. There could be treasure in what you are told. But only you can decide what is best for you.

Chapter Five: Developing Knowledge

In the last chapter we searched for a direction to point our lives. When you have decided on a certain direction, then it is time measure your education and to gather knowledge about your chosen field.

Hiring managers are seeking candidates with the correct mixture of education and training. Believe me, the most powerful lure for the hirer is the applicant who possesses a mixture of Character, Education, and Training. For example, an engineer with good people skills and an understanding of other cultures will command a salary and bonuses several times greater than the engineer who is a great designer, but who cannot be allowed to visit the customer in Europe because he does not do well in social gatherings.

Your quest for knowledge should come before the decision of your direction. Then once you decide on a direction, you gather specialized knowledge of that particular area.

While this specialized knowledge is indispensible, too many job seekers think that if they only get this knowledge or that certification, they will get the job they want. They look at the want ads and say, "I have that license, therefore I'll get hired by this company." They miss the point of there being two types of knowledge: Education and Training.

Education

Your education is comprised of the broad knowledge you've gained in school and through your experiences. Your mother started your education when you were a baby by teaching you a language, how to be courteous, how to play with other children, and the dangers of the dog next door, the cars in the street, and the hot stove.

Later you went to school and took classes that might not have meant so much to you then. But English literature taught you how other people think and feel. History classes showed you the broad movements of the human race, its conflicts, and the achievements of humanity. Mathematics made you think, and speech and writing classes forced you to communicate. Education gives you the lens by which you see the world: Wide or narrow view, focused or warped, clear or clouded by the dust of distractions.

Your interactions on the playground were another type of education. You learned to negotiate, pick teammates, motivate others, and even sometimes fight off the bullies. Life has many more parallels to the playground than to the classroom. We often call this "street smarts".

The hiring manager may not put education in the job requirements, but you can bet he will first probe your resume and correspondence for evidence of your education level.

"Precise writing is the sign of a precise mind."

My writing teacher used to pound that saying into my head over and over. Your writing will be a first impression to many hiring managers. So be careful when you write emails, cover letters, and thank you notes. Get someone to read them over and give you some feedback before you send them.

Later, in the interview, the hiring manager will judge your bearing and posture, the way you speak, your responses to questions, and your body language trying to gauge your education level.

Many hirers place a great deal of weight on a college diploma or advanced degree as evidence of education. But I have met many educated men and women who did not finish university. For whatever reason, lack of funds, desire to start a business, or military service, these people never got around to getting a degree. But they have read the classics, understand people, and have a firm grasp on their central philosophy. One cannot call them "uneducated".

On the other hand, I've met many people with a degree whom one would not call educated. They have no regard for others, do not understand another's viewpoint, and one even bragged that he got his degree without ever reading a book all the way through. These men (almost all have been men) have a distain for those who don't share their religion or philosophy. Anyone different is stupid and/or lazy.

A College Degree and You

If you lack a degree, you will be hindered by most screeners. If you try to go though Human Resources, young people barely out of school will throw out your resume before you have a chance to interview. Do not despair. In later chapters I will show you how to bypass HR (The Hiring Resistance Department).

Some fields require a degree. If you desire to teach at the university level, an advanced degree is mandatory. Other fields, not so much. However, the long term trend is that a university diploma will become mandatory for even entry level corporate positions.

There has never been a time in history where a degree is easier to obtain. I was stationed on an army base in Colombia with another pilot named Jorge. He earned his Master's Degree online at night while flying combat missions over the jungles during the day. You have no excuse. Money problems are easily overcome with loans and grants. Everyone has access to the internet and a library, even prisoners. So, get that degree.

Training

Training, on the other hand, is the specialized knowledge that allows you to perform a certain function in society. Accounting is the knowledge of tracking the flow of assets and liabilities of a person or corporation. Engineering is the understanding of the forces of physics upon man-made structures and appliances.

The trouble with many people in the "hard sciences" such as programming, accounting, engineering, computing, and biology is that they do not recognize that while they have spent many years being trained, their education is usually truncated. Moreover, they denigrate persons who have been educated in history, philosophy, and English.

Another problem highly trained people have is that they often think that since they have excelled in their training, they understand and know all things better than a person in another field. Heart surgeons, CPA's, lawyers, and retired generals seem to fall into this category.

An example of this problem occurred around 1985. NASA computer programmers were working on a new flight routine for the Space Shuttle. As they developed the program, NASA astrophysicists reviewed each maneuver. The two groups fought constantly, and their departments became enemies, so much so that the program ground to a halt.

My brother, who has a Master's Degree in Music Education, was hired as an intermediary to take messages back and forth between the teams. For three months, he listened to both teams. Then he shuttled between buildings, explaining to the programmers how certain maneuvers were impossible, and teaching the astrophysicists the capabilities and limitations of the computer and navigation systems. He was paid well because he could listen and communicate; something that some of the smartest people in the world were unable to do.

Sales Training

Every company needs more trained salespeople. The old saying is still true: "Nothing happens until something is sold." Doctors and bureaucrats don't need to sell. Patients want to get well, so they follow doctors' orders. Bureaucrats have the power of fines and police to get their "customers" to pay. But everyone else needs salesmen.

Architects, lawyers, and accounting firms have salesmen that bring in huge clients. But they don't like to call them "salesmen". They are called "Rainmakers". And they make unholy amounts of money compared to the other professionals in their firm.

There is no faster way to vault into upper management and high income than the sales route. Most people avoid sales, quoting cute sayings like "I couldn't sell a heater to an Eskimo." Excuses won't get you hired in today's economy. The most powerful and desirable applicants are the ones who are both skilled technicians and effective salesmen. If you are an engineer who can sell, you can write your own ticket.

Don't avoid sales. Do you know who the best salesman is in every successful organization?

The CEO.

Track all of the big sales of a corporation and you will find the CEO is the main salesman on the team. When a division or factory is sold, the CEO made the calls and probably the presentation. Customers like to have the president ask them for their business.

One of the best tools of the president of any company is the corporate jet. Here he can have a prospect alone for an uninterrupted hour or two to make his pitch. I've seen it when I have been flying as a corporate pilot. I had one president tell the story of signing an eighty million dollar contract on board his jet. The CEO was the only salesman working that deal, and he closed it on the way home after taking the client to a Dallas Cowboys game. By the way, he said that the profit from that one deal paid for the jet several times over.

Where Can I Get Training?

Training can be obtained in the military, at universities, or through technical schools, corporate training programs, and on the job training. Usually, the training ends with some form of certification and/or license.

I got some of my training in the military, some from technical schools and lots through on the job training. The military cost me four years of service, I borrowed money for my technical school, and the on the job training took many months. Training is never cheap or easy. Almost always, it is more expensive and takes longer than you first imagined.

And remember one thing, training is perishable. I mean that in today's world of ever expanding knowledge, you must continue your education, or your training will become outdated. For example, a surgeon trained a few years ago must return to school every year to learn the new techniques and equipment developed while he was practicing medicine.

This is true for any field, whether it is engineering, law, accounting, or flying an aircraft. During the job interview, the hiring manager will want to see your latest recurrent training or recertification.

Besides being perishable, training is not transferable. My specialized training is flying and maintaining aircraft. This knowledge is not usable in other fields. The eye doctor doesn't care that a King Air 200 aircraft is powered by a Pratt and Whitney PT6A-41 turbine engine. So before we spend money and time gaining specialized knowledge, we must be sure of the field in which we want to work.

However, education is valuable in any field.

The Good News

Both education and training have never been easier to obtain than it is today. With the internet, financial aid, grants, loans and scholarships anyone can get the training and education that he needs.

Schools are recruiting heavily for students and making it easier than ever to afford tuition, books, and living expenses. Just remember, those loans have to be paid back some day.

The military is a great place for a young person to start out. Beware the hidden part of the bargain. The Army will spend hundreds of thousands of dollars teaching you to fly helicopters; the Navy will spend a like amount teaching you to manage nuclear power plants. After his service the Marine rifleman will have his college paid through the GI Bill. However, in return for your training, you will not only have to devote years of service, but you may be required to be separated from your family and perhaps even give your life during wartime.

I've known several of my friends who went back to school to earn degrees even after they married and had children. They worked a job during the day, and went to classes and studied at night. It is not easy, but it is worth it.

What is Your Career Path?

So, as you decide on your direction, be sure to include both education and training. Research your field and learn the "career path" to the top. These career paths are easy to discover. A few minutes talking to someone who is successful in your field will give you all the information you need. Confirm that info with some research on the internet. This should be easy since you have decided on a career that interests you. Be sure to get the normal time span and approximate costs.

Let's take the Career of Professional Pilot and map out the Career Path.

Professional Pilot Career Path

	Cost	Time
Private Pilot License	**$6,000**	**3 months**
Instrument License	**$12,000**	**4 months**
Commercial License	**$9,000**	**6 months**
Gain experience working		**2 years**
Airline Transport License	**$10,000**	**3 weeks**
Gain experience (Advanced Aircraft)		**3 years**

So, you can see that an aspiring pilot will work for several years gaining different licenses and ratings before he earns a decent salary. But do not let that discourage you. Those years of getting experience will be enjoyable because, having chosen a career you enjoy, your work will be like your hobby. The experiences will enrich both your life and your resume.

The career path will look different for a military pilot who might spend up to twenty years in the military before going into the civilian market. Also, some European airlines offer free training to promising candidates in return for a long term employment contract.

By researching your industry, you can find out the same type of information about what types of training and certifications are required, and how long it will take to gain the experience needed to command a good salary.

Start your education and training now, knowing that you will be implementing other parts of this job guide during the process. Gaining the needed diploma or certification might take years, and you will also need to be working on the other strategies mentioned in this book. Life is a mixture of activities. Enjoy gaining knowledge.

Success Story Number Three

(Several of the details have been changed to protect identities.)

Robert Brown got out of the US Army in 1953. He had a new wife and a baby on the way. Using his GI Bill, he enrolled in the University of Mississippi.

His Army benefits only paid for his books and tuition and a small part toward his living expenses, so he worked at a grocery store at night.

Deciding that he wanted to become an officer he entered the ROTC program. On graduation in 1957 with a degree in biology he entered the US Air Force Reserves and was selected for pilot training.

As a Reserve Pilot, he was only required to fly a couple of weekends per month. So he got a job flying the US Mail at night and working in a hospital lab during the day. While working in the hospital, Robert became fascinated with medicine and decided that he wanted to become a medical doctor.

During the next three years, Robert applied to nine medical schools across the south. Each one turned him down because his grades were not that good. But he continued to fly for the Air Force, work two jobs and save.

A friend told him of a medical school opening up in Monterrey, Mexico. So Robert applied, and was accepted. He moved his family to Laredo, Texas. Laredo Air Force Base had a Reserve Squadron where he could still serve as a C-119 pilot on the weekends.

His plan was to attend medical school all week and drive back to Laredo Friday night to see his family. He would fly one or two weekends a month for the flight pay. Then on Sunday night, he would drive back to his tiny apartment in Monterrey for another week of classes.

His only problem was that he only spoke a few words of Spanish. He hired a tutor and studied like a maniac for two months before medical school started.

In two years, he graduated from medical school with a Mexican MD. He applied to the State of Texas and received a Texas license to practice medicine.

Doc Brown was my family doctor and flight surgeon for over twenty-five years.

Doc Brown knew that he needed training to become a medical doctor. He chased that dream for years before it became true. Don't let anything stop you from getting the education and training that you need to get that dream job.

In today's world, it is much easier to obtain training and education that it was for Doc Pate. We have loans, grants, and scholarships available for everything from having outstanding grades to being left handed.

Action Plan

If you are strong on training and weak on education, start in your local library. I know you are grumbling and saying to yourself, "I've had enough of this reading, reading, reading." Growth is always hard. But remember, you are excelling above your competition by doing the work before you get paid. Anyone will work when they are being paid, but the stars, those who get ahead, will work before they get paid.

Check out books on history, concentrating on the area where you think you might work. For example, if you were planning to enter the petroleum industry, the history of Texas, the history of oil exploration, and the history of the modern Middle East would be good books to read first.

Do not neglect some of the classic novels. Ask your librarian for suggestions. Some of my favorites are:

A Tale of Two Cities

The Adventures of Sherlock Holmes

The Count of Monte Cristo

The Sea Wolf

Biographies are another category of books that will guide you and inspire you. Choose great men like Napoleon, Lincoln, and General George Patton. Then narrow down and read biographies of successful people in your field. If you work in computers, read the biographies Michael Dell and Steve Jobs. If you are going into the oil field read the biographies of Armand Hammer and John D. Rockefeller. See what obstacles these men overcame to become successful.

On the other hand, you may be a philosophy major looking to break into the oil business. You know that you lack technical expertise. You should check out:

Nontechnical Guide to Petroleum Geology, Exploration, Drilling and Production

The Prize: The Epic Quest for Oil, Money, and Power

Oil 101

Most community colleges offer night courses in oil field technology. A plus is that many oil companies recruit the top students right from these classes.

You get the idea. Fill in your weak spots. The technical guys need to understand people, the people guys must get a grasp on technology. For most jobs, the technical licenses are a "must have" to get invited to the interview. But once in the interview you **will** be judged on your education level.

Remember, most hiring managers don't understand that they are looking for the perfect mix of education and training in their applicants.

When I have talked to these hirers about why they chose a lesser qualified candidate over another, they spoke of their "gut feelings" about the fully qualified applicant. When I pressed them, they pointed out the little slights like not getting a "thank you" note after the first interview. Some mentioned the poor grammatical structure of the cover letter, or the lack of understanding of the culture of their business.

These managers don't realize that they have an unwritten requirement for character and education built into their interview process. But just because they don't realize it does not diminish its importance.

Let's say that you need a truck to pull a large trailer carrying a backhoe. The trailer weights 19,000 pounds. You put together a list of specifications and email it out to the Ford dealership, the Kenworth store, and the Chevy place asking for bids.

Your list includes:

- Powerful Turbo Diesel Engine
- Heavy duty cooling system
- Six speed towing transmission
- Reinforced frame for towing
- Extra-large brakes
- Dual cab with deluxe seats
- Red paint to match the rest of your fleet.

The Chevrolet bid comes in the cheapest, so you go to the dealership to look over the truck. When the salesman takes you out to the lot, you immediately see that the truck has no tires!

"I've got to have tires," you say.

"Tires were not on your list," the salesman says. "If you'd like tires, you'll have to hire a tire company to install them."

Now isn't that a stupid illustration? Who would try to sell a truck without any tires? But we view hiring the same way. When we prepare ourselves for employment, we try to fit the exact written description of the want ads, and ignore the unwritten requirements.

Businesses must have people who can interact with people, just like the truck owner needs tires. How will the engine transmit its power or the brakes scrub off speed without the tires to grip the pavement? And how will the business communicate its superior technology without someone to explain it to the customers? You must have the mixture of tech and touch that the business needs.

So help the hiring managers love you by developing your optimal mix of education and training. Know etiquette, history of the industry, and some current affairs in addition to having the technical ability to do the job. Every hiring manager wants a person who can:

1) Get the job done.
2) Get along with fellow workers.
3) Be groomed and promoted in the future.

Chapter Six: How to Set Your Goals

Set Goals for Success

You've heard this before, right? Many times you've heard and read that one must set goals to get ahead. Your grandfather probably cornered you years ago and pounded it into your head.

"Without goals you are like a ship without a rudder." I can hear my grandfather saying that as clear as if he were standing here, even though he's been gone for almost thirty years.

So why haven't you set some goals yet? I know why. Goal setting requires some hard, hard work. You must sit down for many hours and think. Thinking is hard. Remember, the wise man acts, even when he doesn't feel like it. The man with a good work ethic works; it is part of his nature.

There is a proper way to set goals and write them out. No, this is not like a magical incantation. But for your brain to act on your goals, you must set certain parameters.

- They must have a specific description.
- They must have a pathway to accomplishment.
- They must have a realistic deadline.
- And they must be within the realm of possibility.

You will use up several sheets writing things that come to mind. Some of you will have your main goal pop up within minutes. Others of you will think and write, then erase and rewrite for perhaps a month before you arrive at your life's goal.

Dedicate an hour or so each day to come up with your central goal.

A Specific Description of Your Goal

In order to have a powerful goal, make a specific goal.

If you write down, "I want to be a professor", you are no better off than if you wrote nothing. Add details.

What kind of professor?

"I want to be a college professor. I like to teach, I enjoy the academic life, and professors earn good money."

Okay. What kind of college professor?

"I want to be a math professor."

At what college or university do you want be a math professor?

"I've always dreamed of being a math professor at Princeton University."

With this statement you now have a specific goal. Do you see how we arrived at that specific goal? Ask yourself questions to get the description down on paper. Narrow it down. The more specific the better.

Remember how we made the list of things you like to do? Let that list of pleasurable activities be your guide. Never before has mankind had so many choices and opportunities. All you have to do is spend some time thinking, really thinking, and then decide where you want to go.

A Pathway to Accomplishment

Now that you have a destination for your journey, how will you proceed?

Just like a road trip, that's how. Let's say we have decided to go to Los Angeles. Before we start, we need to choose the roads we'll take. This is not just so that you have a way to go, but so that you can break down this journey into the smallest parts.

Go to Google Maps and plan a trip. When you print off directions for that trip, the list will have turn-by-turn instructions. Certain actions must be taken before other actions. If you turn right before getting to a certain intersection, you'll end up in the wrong state.

It is the same with your goals. You must break them down into "turn-by-turn" instructions. Down to the point of knowing what to do each day.

Let's continue with our example of becoming a college professor. We have made the goal of being a math professor at Princeton.

What smaller steps must you take to get to that place?

1. I have to earn a PhD in Mathematics.
2. I must be published.

Break down Number One further. What must you do to get a PhD in Mathematics?

A. I need a Bachelor's Degree in Math.
B. I have to earn a Master's Degree in Math.

Break down Number One, A into even smaller pieces.

i. I have to enroll in a Math Program at a university.
ii. I must have some way to pay for tuition and room and board.

Continue to drill into Action Number One, A, i.

a. I must choose a university.

You get the idea. Break down your goal into smaller and smaller pieces until you get to the item that you must do today, this morning, to get started. Your first action toward your dream job may be just a phone call. Make that one step.

Then do something each day that moves you a little closer to that goal. For example, when I decided to become a professional pilot, I researched the industry and found out the path I needed to take.

My first step was to go to the eye doctor and get a waiver for my poor vision. While correctable to 20/20, I couldn't pass the First Class Flight physical wearing my glasses. It would have been stupid for me to start paying for lessons if I couldn't work as a pilot because of my bad vision.

I got new contact lenses in one day and the waiver within a month. I was on my way. I've been a pro pilot since 1982.

Make Your Goal Big Enough

Too many times, I have seen the unemployed willing to work far below their capabilities. Yes, you will probably have to take a lower job as you work toward your ultimate goal. I'm not talking about that.

I see many capable people settling for a position way too low. They won't even consider that they could get a top paying position, so they don't prepare themselves and they don't seek out interviews. And yet, these top positions are often the slots that are the hardest for senior management to fill.

When you set your goal, aim high. Now not all of you want to be a manager or an owner. I understand that. However, if you are an auto mechanic, wouldn't you rather work at a prestigious dealership earning $100k per year instead of a tune-up shop making $40k?

I am a pilot, so I set my sights to work at the company with the highest pay outside of the Iraq/Afghanistan region. And after a couple of years, I got there. So now, for flying the same type of aircraft, I am earning nearly three times the pay of other pilots.

Analyze what you must do to get the higher positions. For technical positions, you probably need to become a Subject Matter Expert (SME). You will also need some communication skills to transmit that knowledge in writing and public speaking.

You can become an expert by studying technical manuals and industry regulations. Both types of information can be obtained on the internet or at the library.

For a people oriented position, you must be able to teach, mentor, and persuade the people under your care. Books on psychology, motivation, and management theory would be a good place to start your preparation.

Often overlooked are the sales positions. Many salesmen bring in more money than management. For several years I did very well selling aircraft. A top salesman needs both a good technical background and people skills. Know your product and understand your prospect. Don't dismiss the sales route. There is no quicker way to a big income and the executive suite. Yes, selling is hard work. Yes, you must deal with rejection.

Some of the world's biggest billionaires started out in sales. H. Ross Perot set sales records for IBM. Wayne Huizenga (founder of Waste Management, Inc.) collected garbage early in the mornings, and went door to door in the afternoons signing up clients. My life insurance salesman earns over $250,000 a year. I talked to the salesman that sold us a new mattress last month. He earns $120,000. For a quick start towards financial success, take a good look at selling.

Aim high and start your preparation. Remember the words of the ancient Roman philosopher, Seneca.

"Luck happens when opportunity meets preparedness."

Success Story Number Four

(Some names, places, and dates have been changed to protect the people in this story.)

On a foggy morning in May of 1979, a helicopter pilot working for a coal company in Kentucky crashed into a mountain, dying instantly. Perhaps he was distracted thinking of his sick wife, and how was he going to afford to keep sending his son to university. Added to that, his son wanted to take flying lessons and become a professional pilot.

The pilot's son, Anthony Meyers, was about to graduate from the local community college, and wanted to go on and get his four year degree at State. When the son came home that day, he saw all the cars around his house, and knew that something was terribly wrong. He ran in thinking that his mother had died. But it was not his mother.

After struggling through the funeral and her grief, Anthony's mother told him of her financial condition. There was no life insurance, so he couldn't go to university, and she forbade him to become a pilot like his father. It was December, 1979, and horribly cold.

So he left home. But Anthony had a plan. He would move to where flying was active, work around aircraft and earn his pilot's license. Then one day he would be a professional pilot.

With the few hundred dollars of savings he had, Anthony hitchhiked to Texas. The recession was on, but he heard that aviation was still doing well on the Texas/Mexico border. Besides, it was warm down there.

Arriving in McAllen, Texas, Anthony rented a tiny apartment, bought a used bicycle, and applied to be an aircraft fueler at Upper Valley Aviation. The clean cut young man was hired instantly.

For the next two years, Anthony worked fueling freight aircraft at night, saving every nickel. He took a flying lesson when he could afford one, gradually building up toward his private pilot's license. He had no TV. He had no stereo. He had no phone. In July, 1982, he passed his private pilot checkride.

That is when he and I started working together. That August I had just gotten my first job as a pro pilot flying a single engine Cessna 206 for an exclusive hunting and fishing lodge in Northern Mexico. I made daily runs from McAllen down to the lodge carrying groceries, generator and tractor parts, ice, canned soft drinks, and hardware.

Each time I landed, I was given another shopping list. I worked 18 hour days, but it was alright because I was paid by the trip. One after-noon, I fell asleep at the controls, and woke up with the aircraft in a spiral toward the ground. I had no problem keeping awake for the 45 minutes home.

As I parked the plane and shut down, Anthony came up to me to get my fuel order.

"Hey, would there ever be any chance that I could ride along and build up some hours?" he asked.

You see, Anthony needed two hundred flight hours before he would be ready to start on his instrument license. Since he couldn't afford to purchase those hours, he rode right seat with the freight guys whenever he could and logged the time that he actually manipulated the controls.

This was a God-sent blessing for me. I was making $6,000 a month in 1982 dollars. I didn't want to slow down.

"Yes sir! I have one more flight today. Can you go with me?"

An hour and a half later, we left McAllen carrying a thousand pounds of ice for the lodge. The lodge needed lots of ice for the customers. They used it in their drinks, and filled their coolers to keep beer cold going out to hunt, and to keep the dead birds cool coming back.

Being on generator power, making ice at the lodge just took too much energy. Besides, the water was bad. I could load up a thousand pounds of crushed ice, fly it for an hour and a half in the cool of the evening, and deliver 900 pounds to the camp.

Anthony flew, and I slept. We unloaded in San Fernando, Mexico and landed back in McAllen at 9 pm. Anthony got 2.5 hours flight time, and I got two and a half hours of sleep.

We met again at 4 am to start the next day.

I called him my "Organic Autopilot". He also helped me shop for the items on my list and helped load and unload the plane. Whenever I offered him money, he declined. "The flight time is pay enough," he'd say.

Anthony got between 5 and 7 hours of flight time per day, except for Wednesday and Thursday, our days off. During those three months Anthony got his 200 hours.

Over the next two years Anthony earned his instrument and commercial pilot's licenses. In addition, he taught himself Spanish. He checked out books from the library and practiced speaking with everyone he thought spoke Spanish.

He still went on trips with me since I was working as a part-time corporate pilot and selling aircraft. Sometimes I would hire him to ferry aircraft I had bought or to deliver aircraft I had sold.

The next fall, 1985, he got hired as the pilot for the hunting lodge where I started. He made enough money to move to a nicer apartment and buy a used car. He still had no TV.

Anthony worked as an aircraft fueler, then part-time pilot, and one day he was hired as the pilot for a small law firm. They only paid him for the days he flew, so he never made really good money with them.

On a spring day in May, 1993, Anthony was drinking coffee in the pilot's lounge at the private aircraft terminal. A nice corporate Cheyenne taxied in, ordered fuel, and the captain asked if anyone was familiar with going in and out of Mexico.

Their corporation had just bought a giant bra factory in Matehuala, Mexico, and they were taking top management down there.

"Sure, I can help you," Anthony said. They went into the flight planning room and Anthony briefed the pilots on everything they would need. Since the corporation hadn't purchased the correct insurance for Mexico, Anthony took the captain downtown to purchase a one week policy.

By the time they returned, the captain had hired Anthony for three days to go down with them as their translator. They paid well. As the months went by, this corporation hired Anthony more and more often.

In December, 1993, this corporation offered him a full time position, to include flight training as captain in their smallest corporate jet. Suddenly, Anthony leapfrogged to the top of the corporate pilot heap. In a couple of years, he was making over 100k, plus a generous benefits package.

It took Anthony Meyers 14 years to go from an aircraft fueler to a corporate jet captain.

Most people would have said that life dealt Anthony a bad hand. No money, no college education, no encouragement from his family. Many people close to him, such as his girlfriend, told him that the goal he set in 1979, to become a corporate pilot, was just impossible. Everyone knew that it cost upwards of $60,000 to get the training to be a corporate pilot.

But Anthony stuck with his plan. He had the wisdom to know that sowing the seed and tending his field would produce a harvest. He had the patience to wait, and the wisdom and discipline to spend his money on training and not on cars, electronics, computers, or beer.

It was Anthony's character that got him that job. He was hired before many other applicants with much more experience and training because Anthony is a good and generous person. Plus he worked hard to learn Spanish, making himself a more valuable candidate.

A foolish person will scoff at this advice. They don't understand the power of the human spirit.

Watch out for your friends. They will be a constant distraction.

"Life is too short to work that hard. You've got to enjoy life now. Have a beer," your buddies will tell you. Don't listen to that. You know in your heart that time is ticking away. Invest in yourself.

Setting goals is not a onetime event. You will find that you are constantly refining your set of objectives. This is not to say that you are wishy-washy, but you must remain flexible.

Let's go back to our example of a trip from New York City to Los Angeles. You have planned out your route, you have the money that you need, and you start the journey. In Ohio, you come to a bridge that has been washed away by a flood. You consult your map, and then change your route and dip south into Kentucky and then continue westward.

This is reasonable. On a journey we might change our route four or five times for construction, a desire to see a landmark, or even a snow storm. We could be delayed due to car trouble. But we continue the journey.

Why don't we think this way about our like goals? Yet with one detour, most people discard their goal.

Society is littered with individuals who tell their tales of woe.

"I could have been successful except the interest rates went up, and I couldn't afford to stay in business."

"I would have been a millionaire if not for my mother getting sick and dying. After that, I just couldn't go on."

Since I am a pilot, this is the one that I hear the most.

"I was going to be a pilot, but I couldn't see putting in all that time and money into training, and then work one of those entry level jobs making $19,000 a year."

But you will be different. You understand that life will throw down obstacles in your path. When you meet those barriers you will choose to go over or around it. But don't stop. Adjust your plans. Pull out the paper and pen and adjust your goals. Redo your pathway and reset your timeline.

You may face a delay, but never give up.

During the depths of the depression, J. Paul Getty bought some beachfront property in Mexico. In fact he bought most of the real estate surrounding this sleepy little Mexican town. Before he could finish the resort he was building, World War II came along. Mr. Getty did well with his oil business in the war, but his resort languished.

Several times, his accountants advised him to sell the Mexican property for a loss. But J. Paul Getty wanted another business besides oil. He wanted to diversify, and so he waited out the war. In 1950, after a nearly fifteen year delay, he opened his resort and publicized the little town of Acapulco, which became the greatest tourist destination in Mexico in the '50's and '60's. As you know, he made another fortune.

J. Paul Getty had a goal. But due to the war, he had to revise his goal shifting the timeline to the right, as you project managers would say. Don't let a delay or some circumstance derail your plan. Adjust, improvise, and overcome.

Another Thing to Think About

In the Success Story above, Anthony changed his location. A severe recession gripped most of the country at the time, but he had heard that aviation was going strong in South Texas. So Anthony moved.

Step back and take a good look at your location. By that, I mean, what are the business opportunities in your area?

Is your area growing? My guess is that you are reading this book because you are unemployed or underemployed. Is that because your town is going through tough times? Has a big factory closed or are more folks moving out than are moving in?

Conditions change, and you must change with them or be crushed. Our forefathers left all to come to the New World. And we have benefited from their courage and foresight.

Use your wisdom to see past the emotional ties you have to a certain place. Are you in a small town? Opportunities are limited if your community's population is under 100,000.

Conrad Hilton, the great hotelier, started showing his entrepreneurial skills while running his father's general store and hotel in San Antonio, New Mexico, a tiny village on the Rio Grande near Socorro, NM. The year was 1918. A multi-millionaire named Charles B. Eddy was in town, and he spent a couple of nights in the little hotel in the center of town.

Conrad wanted to hear how the man had managed to build railroads, develop mines, and grow his businesses. Hilton caught the bearded gentleman sitting on the hotel porch in the cool of the evening. He walked up and confidently asked the old man's secret. The reply stayed with Hilton for over seventy years:

"Son, if you're going to launch big ships,

You've got to go where the water is deep."

Conrad took that advice, and moved to the oil fields of West Texas. In just a few months, Conrad Hilton opened his first hotel in the oil boom town of Cisco, Texas. A couple of years later, he opened a high rise hotel in Abilene, Texas. Then Dallas. Well, you know the rest. Today Hilton is an international hotel chain.

Mr. Hilton told this story hundreds of times during his 91 years. You see, Mr. Eddy saw immediately the limitations of Hilton remaining in his home town. When Conrad told his mother about the talk, she encouraged him to leave New Mexico and seek his fortune. She knew that if he stayed in that tiny New Mexico town, that he would never have the opportunities of a bigger place.

I've talked with educated, employable men and women who would not leave a dying town because of emotional attachments. That decision is up to you. But don't complain when financial disaster sneaks up and crushes you. While you have some savings and some time, move to a city with economic growth.

You don't try to start a palm tree nursery in Alaska, and you don't offer snow skiing lessons in Florida. Why will you insist on seeking a job where none exist?

Our ancestors moved because of war, famine, and persecution. They kept their families fed and continued their line. Shouldn't we be willing to move to "deep water" where there is more opportunity?

Let's look at your list again.

You have broken your goals down to their smallest parts. You know what you must do and the way you must go to arrive at your destination. Now we are going to assign periods of time to accomplish each of those major steps so that you can:

Set a Realistic Timeline

A realistic timeline is so important, and yet it is almost always left off. For example: If you want to write a novel, it is fantasy to put down a timeline of three weeks. Even a practiced and prolific writer like Steven King takes six months or more to deliver a manuscript to his publisher.

On the other hand, understand that you have certain gateways. In our example above where you want to be a math professor, you know that if you don't get enrolled in a university by September, you will lose several months until you have a chance to enroll again. Sometimes you must be patient and sometimes you must hurry.

Research your goal and understand what it will take in terms of time and resources before you write down a timeline. If your goal is to become a math professor at Princeton, it will take at least seven years to get your PhD in Mathematics plus a few years as a professor in a lesser university before you will be ready for Princeton.

Don't be afraid of a goal that has a timeline of many years. If you are doing something that you enjoy, as we talked about at the first of the chapter, then you will be having a great time along the way!

In the last section, we broke your goal down into tiny pieces. Take each of those pieces and assign how much time it should take to accomplish that piece. Even our Google driving directions have a certain number of minutes assigned to each road section.

How can you know if you are staying on track unless you keep score? Time is one of the scores you will keep.

What is Your View of Time?

Time has different values for each of us. But I will tell you that the rich have a different view of time than the poor. All you need to do is look up the mountain of research about this characteristic of the rich.

All of that research can be boiled down to this statement: The longer the timeframe of the planner, the more successful they are. In other words, a poor man might just be looking for his next meal. He scrambles around and finds a day job sweeping a warehouse. He works all day for $45 cash. With money in his pocket, he's happy.

The successful person might be just as broke and hungry. (Rich people don't always have money. But they always have a plan to earn more.) Let's say our rich man shows up at the same cleanup site. But he has a plan:

Find some work.   [Today]

Do a great job and get on full time.   [This week.]

Save my money and get training.   [One year.]

Go to school at night.   [Two years.]

Become a technician.   [Three years.]

Move up into management.   [Ten years.]

Own my own company.   [Fifteen years]

The only difference between the two men in our example is that one has set goals. He has broken those goals down into the smallest pieces—down to what he must do today. And finally, he has assigned a time line. Now he possesses more than a goal: He has a **PLAN.**

If we fast forward a few years, we will see the poor man still scrambling around trying to find a little work here and there. Or perhaps he's found a full time job as a fork lift driver.

By contrast, the rich man will be in senior management earning four times the money. He will be saving like crazy to either start or buy his own business. He is still following his plan. Over the years he has had to modify that plan, but he's still on track.

The poor look at the rich, and say, "Man, they are lucky. They are an overnight success."

But the poor don't realize that the rich make their luck through wisdom, goal setting, and hard work. And like my father says:

> **"It usually takes about twenty years to become an overnight success."**

Your Goals Must Be Within the Realm of Possibility

In the last few pages I have been spouting that you can accomplish your dream. But now, I want to bring you to earth for just a moment. As you plan out your life and set your goals, make sure your central goal is a possibility.

For example, I have always wanted to be a fighter pilot. But like I told you, I have weak eyes and must wear glasses or contact lenses to get to 20/20. I don't qualify for military pilot training.

Now, I could hire a lawyer, lobby Congress, and organize protests to get the Air Force to change their requirements for fighter pilots. But is that realistic? Will the Air Force change to accommodate me? I don't think so. Not reasonable.

Or let's say I want to become an NFL quarterback. I am 55 years old. No matter how hard I train, or how many times I apply to different teams, I will not become an NFL quarterback. I'm too old. I have no experience as a football player, much less as a quarterback.

However, if I set my sights on becoming a successful businessman, I can accomplish that. Colonel Sanders didn't start his chicken franchise, Kentucky Fried Chicken, until he was in his sixties.

So while you can and should set big goals, make them realistic. Remember, the man of wisdom doesn't try to jump off of a building and fly; he earns good money so that he can buy a helicopter.

Post Your Goals

The human is a forgetful creature, and the daily grind can push your goals out of your remembrance. So, lots of life coaches recommend posting your goals. Some put their goals on the mirror in the bathroom.

I know one novelist who has his goals scrolling across his computer screen as his screensaver. The one that stays on his monitor the longest is:

A Writer Has Written Today.

I have made a movie about my goals and I watch that movie several times a week. It has pictures representing my goals with the goals printed at the bottom. The music is inspiring, and I always feel invigorated after watching.

But you must also keep in mind the timeline. Review your timeline each month. Make new lists of things to do today. And keep on track.

Exercise Number Four

Each business day, put on the business attire that you purchased in Exercise Number Two. Go out and talk with people. One day, go to the donut shop, one day to the library, one day to a museum. But go somewhere and talk with people.

Practice striking up a conversation. Introduce yourself and hand out your business cards. Practice listening and find out about people. If you can, give your new acquaintance some good piece of information. They may be looking for a good auto repair shop, or need a lawyer.

Let people know a little bit about your goals. No details, but tell them that you are going to school to become a mathematics professor, if that is your dream.

If you can, point the people you meet toward someone in your network. Practice generosity. Most of all make it your goal to connect with someone each day. I'm not saying that you have to become best friends, but you should gain some small piece of understanding about each other.

You can do this exercise either before or after an errand or an interview. It needn't take more than a half hour.

Chapter Seven: Developing your Network

In order to accomplish your goals, you must work with people. No matter how smart or talented you are, without a team, you will go nowhere. Even if you are brilliant and a fantastic worker, without a network no one will forward your ideas, no one will invest in you, and no one will want to have you around.

A Mutual Support Society

On the other hand, when you have a powerful network, you never lack for opportunities. Because you have given referrals and info to your network, made recommendations and introductions, and done favors when presented with the opportunity, the members of your network will reflect that back on you.

You will be able to call people in your network to get all types of inside information from who's the best surgeon to who's got money and is looking for an investment opportunity in a start-up business. You'll know the best restaurants in town and how to get tickets to the big game when no one else can.

Don't dismiss this. Working with people is the greatest skill. Executives are not the best engineers, but they can get the best out of their engineers. A business owner may not know all that his chief of maintenance knows about machinery, but the owner knows how to employ the knowledge of that chief of maintenance and how to build good will and loyalty in his people.

Look for Win-Win Situations

I worked with an inventor about ten years ago and wrote a business plan for his new invention. This inventor is responsible for some well-known inventions, but he never made any money from them other than a salary from the lab where he worked.

He believed that the whole world was out to cheat him, and he loudly proclaimed that belief to all. He was rude, unreasonable, and greedy for money. After a while I stopped working with him, even though he had a breakthrough invention. He had never developed any people skills.

In pure technology, this man was probably the smartest person I've ever known. Yet he lost his house in foreclosure while he sat on a design for a revolutionary generator and air conditioner. But he could never sell his designs because he would not trust anyone. He would not sign any agreement where another party would benefit "too much". I tried to explain to him that in order for a deal to work, all sides had to benefit.

The inventor died a couple of years ago, flat broke, but still owning the patents to his two greatest inventions.

On the other hand, men of much less intelligence have become wildly successful by setting up and maintaining a large and loyal network of other humans. In these networks the members trust and support each other, funneling work and information to those in the network who can use it.

The members of these networks want to see their friends profit. Jealousy and envy have no place in a successful network. You see, developing a network is an exercise in **Generosity**. You recognize that as part of Character that we discussed in Chapter Two, don't you?

I wish I had understood the power of Networking when I was younger. I've lost track of hundreds of friends, relatives, Army buddies, and business contacts. Each is a valuable human being. Not only will your network bring you business opportunities and jobs, it will enrich your life in ways that you would never imagine. So we'll start to build a network together, and you will soon see the power I'm talking about.

How to Build Your Network

Just like building a house, you need a plan, and then you need to work that plan. Networking can be enjoyable, but it is also work. We have new tools today, but the process is the same. Thousands of years ago our ancestors started with just being able to network face to face. Then they wrote letters and cards.

Starting in the 1850's our forefathers sent cables by signal flags from tower to tower between cities, and then by telegram. In the 1890's along came the telephone. The next big step up was email. Now we have Facebook, Twitter, and texting.

We need to do all of these things today. But be assured that the most powerful tools you have are face-to-face meetings and handwritten notes. Why do you think that corporations and nations spend such huge amounts of money to move leaders around in private jets? Because face-to-face meetings are the most powerful and productive tool of any leader. Never forget this.

Part One: Gather Your Contacts

Make lists of all your contacts. Start with relatives, friends, business associates, doctors, bankers, and anyone else you can think of.

After you have that list together, look for other lists. How about your high school graduating class? You can look them up on the internet. One of your old buddies might be a valuable contact.

List your friends at church. What about your neighbors? Use your imagination. Where did you go to university? Contact the alumni association to reconnect with professors and fellow graduates.

Dig through your drawers. If you are like me, you have a couple of hundred business cards from conventions and meetings, from old customers and employers. Add them to your list.

Don't forget your email contacts and your friends on Facebook, Twitter, and the other social networks.

Do you see the pattern here? Gather your assets. You truly have gold scattered around your house. Find the nuggets and assemble them.

Now that you have piles of business cards, printouts of alumni, lists written on scraps of paper, old Christmas and birthday cards, it is time to consolidate your names onto a master list. Some people use computers, some use card files or rolodexes. It doesn't matter so much what type of medium you use as long as you get your list together.

I use a popular internet mail provider since I know that all my contacts are saved on their servers. I don't have to worry about a hard drive crashing, a stolen laptop. Or losing a rolodex to a fire, or going on a trip and forgetting to bring it along.

Part Two: Reconnect With Your Contacts

Our master list is never finished. You add to it day by day. But using what you have so far, it's time to start working. Pick one or two contacts a day to catch up with. For your best contacts, plan a lunch or breakfast together. Phone others. And email the rest.

A powerful way to connect with those on your list is to send out hand written cards at the appropriate times. If you hear that one of your friends won an award, send him a card of congratulations. Of course, you **must** send out "thank you" notes to any of your contacts who have helped you. Even CEO's of giant corporations know they must spend part of their week writing "thank you" notes.

When you read or hear about a relative of a contact passing away, send a sympathy card. The unexpected hand-written note letting your friend know how you are doing is also powerful.

I just stopped writing at the end of the last paragraph to reconnect with an old buddy. Remember my story in Chapter One about getting the contract to dig holes to check fiber optic cables? I wanted to see how Don McDonald was doing and thank him once again for the help he gave me at a low time in my life.

None of his phone numbers worked, so I googled his name, only to find out that he died of a massive heart attack eight years ago. I feel terrible that I lost contact with a man who helped me so much 15 years ago. Don't let this happen to you.

When you reconnect with your contacts do not ask them for help finding a job. First you must refill your personal bank accounts.

Let me explain.

In every relationship, there is a bank account. And believe me both sides of the friendship instinctively know the balance of that bank account. Every time you help the other person, you deposit into the account that exists between the two of you. The deposit can take the form of a sincere "Thank you," a compliment, a favor, or a piece of news that helps the other person.

Each time you snub the other person, don't return phone calls or fail to acknowledge a death in their family, there is a withdrawal from your account. If you have not contacted that person in a while, you probably have a big deficit.

So our first mission is to rebuild our account balances. We do this by calling our siblings, parents, and cousins. Reconnect with old friends. Don't eat alone. Each day invite someone over for lunch or a cup of coffee. You don't need to spend much money or more than an hour a day doing this, but it will pay off big.

The temptation for the job seeker is to pick out people in your lists who are rich and powerful and able to help immediately. Don't go down that path. Number one, it is transparent. The rich and powerful got rich and powerful by understanding other's motivations. They will know exactly what you are trying to do and feel like you are just using them. So it won't work.

Number Two, it is cynical and selfish. Remember, we are striving to improve our character first, and then our intangible assets. Your network is one of those intangibles, but if you sacrifice your character to build your network, you sacrifice the greater to gain the lesser. And ironically, you will end up driving people from your network if your contacts get even a hint that they are just being used for your benefit.

Exercise Number Five

It's time to get to work on your network. Gather your lists together and call or visit people in your network that you have not contacted in over three months.

Just chat with them. If it comes up, tell them that you are looking for work. But don't ask them for help. It's not the right time. It will appear that you just called to ask for help. That is not what networks are for.

End your visit with the following question:

"Is there anything I can do for you?"

If your friend asks for something, move heaven and earth to get it done. Be generous first, and then you will receive.

Exercise Review

1. You are finding some type of work to do every day. Remember that you are a hard worker. Workers work every day. (Your wife will love this!)
2. Every work day you get up, shave, wash, and dress in business attire.
3. Seek career advice from a respected source or a coach.
4. You are mingling in the community, and handing out your business card. Be helpful.
5. Every day you contact, preferably in person, one or two people in your network.

Part Three: Adding New Members to Your Network

I hope you have made it this far in the book. Many people find a job after just contacting a few people from their past. Several times, when I have been unemployed, just a couple of phone calls have resulted in a job offer.

I hope that you have gotten the job of your dreams. But don't stop building your network. The tool we call Networking will bring so much good into your life, not to mention promotions and opportunities.

You have gotten your list together; you have visited a few, called many, and emailed the rest. Now is the time to expand your network into the upper reaches of business. I have found several effective and inexpensive ways to get make real connections with the top decision makers.

Develop Your "Elevator Speech"

When you meet new people, they will ask you what you do for a living. You have only a few seconds to make a good impression. You want each person you meet to see you in your best light. Having a thirty second speech that is informative and concise will make you look focused and knowledgeable.

The Elevator Speech is named so because you should be able to meet someone in an elevator and give them an accurate message of your goals and/or business before you reach the top floor.

Write out your elevator speech and practice it. This will be your thirty second commercial. If you are still a student, list your education level, your major, and your ultimate goal.

Student Example

"My name is Pete Julius. I am a junior at Minnesota State University, majoring in business and minoring in Spanish. And I'm looking for a summer internship in a medium sized manufacturing business."

Business Example

"Hi, I'm Joan Figueroa. I have fourteen years experience in office administration. In my last position, I was the office manager of a corporation grossing $28 million in sales. Seven administrative assistants worked under my direction in both Accounts Receivable and Accounts Payable. I'm seeking a position as a personal assistant to a CEO level executive. My best strengths are loyalty, attention to detail, and competitive intelligence."

I think you can see what I mean. Write out at least three different versions of your elevator speech, and then pick the best one. Practice in front of a mirror until you have your elevator speech down cold. This way when you bump into the CEO of Mega Corp at the next convention you won't stumble. Don't laugh. These things do happen, and if you are prepared, you could be hired or referred on the spot. I've seen it.

Join the Rotary Club

This is my favorite group, but it can be the Kiwanis, or the Elk's Lodge, or the Odd Fellows. You may have friends at one or the other. Or there may only be one of these groups close to your home. The reason I chose the Rotary Club is that it seems packed with people from upper management and owners of local companies. If you are hunting, you need to go where the deer are.

These clubs are dedicated to helping others. Some, like the Shriners, provide burn care and orthopedic hospitals for children. Others do good work in the community such as funding parks, hospitals, or sending traveling doctors to Africa. There are too many good things they do to list even a part of them here. One of the best boosts for your career is to join one of these organizations. Attend regularly.

The next piece of advice has drawn the most howls from my coaching clients. In most of these clubs they have a speaker every week who gives a talk on some subject they feel passionate about. As soon as you can, you should volunteer to be one of these speakers. This will get you noticed.

Prepare and practice your speech. **Do not read the speech.** Also use little or no Power Point slides. Communicate and connect with your audience.

If you are not a good public speaker, get the book:

Speak Like Churchill, Stand Like Lincoln:
21 Powerful Secrets of History's Greatest Speakers,
by James C. Humes.

This little book is the best I have ever read on becoming a competent and powerful speaker. Your talk can be on your profession, your experiences, your vision for the future of your industry, or an opportunity to serve.

Avoid political rants, religious themes, and subjects not related to business or the humanitarian goals of the club. Above all, do not be boring.

Remember the Call to Action.

Your speech must end with a call to action. Otherwise, why speak unless you wish to change the hearer. If you speak about business accounting, talk about the benefits the accountant brings to the business: tax advice, profit maximization, and a clear picture of its financial condition. At the end of your speech ask the hearers to respect their accountants and seek the account's opinion before any big business decision.

The Call to Action gives your speech its power and impact. Seek to change your audience just a little.

I can hear your protests even as I pound this out on my keyboard.

"I didn't sign up for giving a speech! Won't happen. No way."

The US Army did a study years ago which concluded that the average soldier preferred to be shot at during a firefight than to be forced to speak in public. I don't know why humans have such an ingrained fear of speaking in front of others. But the fear is real.

Remember back when we were talking about developing your character and your intangible assets? Public speaking is a multi-pronged tool to develop and display the following characteristics:

1. **Courage.** You must have courage to stand before a crowd and hold forth about some subject.
2. **Confidence.** Just by asking for the speaking slot, you demonstrate confidence in your ability.
3. **Preparation.** When you speak well, it shows that you have thought about, planned, prepared, and then delivered your message with power and grace.
4. **Knowledge.** Your presentation will demonstrate how you've made yourself an expert in some corner of your field.
5. **The Power of Persuasion.** When you are able to connect with your hearers and move them toward your point of view, that is power-- that is leadership.

After your first speech, you will be viewed in a much different light than before. Believe me, there will be business leaders in your audience who will be thinking:

> **"This person could be a valuable addition to my team. I'm going to watch him. I'll have to get to know him better."**

As soon as you finish, you will know you've been effective if some of the members come up and talk with you, perhaps asking questions about your talk. Be sure to have business cards to hand out.

I have a friend named Steve who took this approach and it resulted in a whole different outcome than he forecast. Steve figured that he would give a speech and then get hired as a sales manager, the position he had held with another company.

Instead, one of the members of his club came up and asked Steve to give his speech at the member's sales meeting the next Monday. Steve agreed, thinking this would be a good way into the corporation.

"We can only pay you a $500 speaking fee."

Steve tried to keep the surprise off of his face. This fee led to a nice side business of public speaking. He still gives speeches and classes even after accepting an offer as a real estate broker with another firm.

From there, watch for the next big push by your charitable organization. All of these clubs have an annual or semi-annual activity to raise money or serve the community.

I have seen the Kiwanis sponsor and provide security for a mini-Grand Prix race through downtown, the Lions collect used eyeglasses and contributions to send eye doctors to poor countries, and the Shriners perform in parades to publicize their children's hospitals.

Your goal is to become involved in your club's activity. You should be involved because it is the right and generous thing to do. But also, this gives you a chance to get to know executives who you would never be able to meet otherwise. Volunteer for a leadership job. These organizations always have problems filling these slots. Not only will the members appreciate your hard work, but you will have an instant showcase for your abilities.

Once you volunteer, you will meet with planning committees, arrange for financing and/or donations, check on insurance, sign up other members, organize publicity, and a hundred other things. These committees will be chock full of executives from your community. These executives will notice your hard work, dependability, and problem solving skills.

Next comes the activity itself. During the big push, you will show up early, handle minor emergencies, be friendly and smile a lot. You will stay late and help clean up. The major benefit you will receive is that you will help other people. You will gain confidence and self respect.

More than one person has been hired for a top management slot based upon his performance during one of these volunteer activities. The executive knows that if you can help plan and manage a project successfully without pay, you should do even better when it is part of your paying job.

Get a Mentor

Service organizations such as Rotary or Elks are the perfect place to search out a Mentor. A mentor is a guide, a counselor, a tutor who can help you around the most troubling places in your career. Even more, he is the one who can intercede for you, using his influence to persuade an employer to hire you for a top position.

For centuries older men and women understood the duty and pleasure of guiding a young person along the paths of their chosen vocation. But somehow that has fallen out of the common career path. I can remember being told in the Army that the work of an experienced soldier is never complete until that soldier has trained another to take his place.

Some say that the competitive nature of today's business world keeps the experienced ones from telling their secrets. Or is it because young people show distain for the wisdom of the elders? I think it is a little of both.

But you are different. Remember, you are a man or woman of wisdom. You can see the value of talking to one who has already walked the path you have chosen.

As a young pilot, I wanted a job flying a heavy freight aircraft. Jim Kemp, one of the older pilots had flown a little with me in helicopters. Plus, he was a retired Army 82nd Airborne paratrooper (one of several who have helped me). Taking me on as his "project", he convinced the owner to hire me to fly copilot on a heavy freight aircraft when I only had 500 hours total flight time. The company minimum was 2,500 hours. Not only was it a big boost to my wallet, but the experience was invaluable.

How do you find and engage a mentor?

1. **Be good at your profession.** A mentor wants to sponsor someone who is capable. He will see the good of helping you and the benefit of introducing you to his network.
2. **Be humble and willing to learn.** When you show true respect for your mentor's knowledge and accomplishments, he will be more willing to give you instruction and help.
3. **Ask.** How will your prospective mentor know that you would like some help unless you communicate that to him? Be tactful and respectful, but ask for help. As always, it is better to ask after you have helped him with something he cares about. That is why the service club route is such a good way to meet your new mentor.

Join a Networking Club

Probably the best way to turbocharge the membership of your network is to join a networking club. All across the nation, there are groups of individuals who recognize the value of a good network. These folks meet once a week, usually around 7 am, before work, to get to know each other and share referrals.

A retired Special Forces soldier decided to start an "Adventure Travel" business taking small groups of rich folks to climb mountains, swim with whales, and scuba dive historical shipwrecks. His business languished until he joined one of these networking clubs.

At first he gave referrals freely, but got nothing back. Gradually, and then in spurts, the group connected him with clients. Soon he was swamped with business, and became so busy that he doubled his fees to thin the crowd. But he still had too many clients. So he doubled the fees again.

Needless to say, he made some good money from his business until he was recruited as a Private Military Contractor.

There are groups that you can join that cost money, others are free, and I know folks that have started their own. Most networking groups have a few things in common.

1. They meet together regularly to share referrals.
2. The group is normally less than thirty people.
3. The membership is diversified. Some even have limits of only one or two of any one type of profession. (You can imagine what a networking club full of engineers would be like.) Instead there is a mixture of salesmen, plumbers, computer geeks, eye doctors, authors, and oil men.
4. Members must give out referrals. If a member is slack about giving out referrals, then he is asked to leave to make room for another.
5. Each member takes his turn giving a five to ten minute speech about his business. Usually only two or three speakers per meeting.
6. Business cards and brochures are handed out and each member displays other members' material in his place of business.

Networking groups work if you work them. In other words, join, attend, and give out referrals. Don't keep score. Be generous, and the referrals will come pouring in.

Chapter Eight: Preparing for the Interview

"But we haven't even talked about getting an interview. How are we going to prepare for something we haven't gotten yet?" You ask a good question.

A boxer does not begin to prepare for a fight only after his agent has booked one, does he? A singer does not wait until he has a gig to start practicing and memorizing his songs. Neither should you wait.

Interviewing is the performance section of the job seeker's manual. You have worked so hard for so long just to get the interview. But when you stand in front of the person or board with the power to hire, if you flub it, you'll still be without a job. So you must prepare. Remember, success comes from the inside. You must upgrade your character and your intangible assets to score big on an interview.

The normal job seeker works for weeks or even months to get an interview with their dream company. Then, after they have an appointment, they start to prepare. In the space of days or perhaps a week, these regular job seekers cram for possibly the biggest day of their career.

WRONG.

You must start to prepare now, before the interview. Even if you think your interview will be in another six months. The better prepared you are, the more likely that the hirer will no longer question whether his company can use you. Instead, he will be asking, "What will it take for you to come to work for us?"

Then you can get right to negotiating salary and bonus.

To prepare for the interview, you must understand why a company hires people and their hiring process. You must understand the attitude of the interviewer, and you must know the gateways you will be expected to pass through.

Why Do Companies Hire People?

Listening to some of my unemployed friends, one would think that companies exist to hire the unemployed for the good of society. These jobless friends are incensed when a local company hires someone who is already employed at another company or firm.

"He should have hired someone without a job. Don't they know that people are suffering out here?"

Why are my friends upset? Because they don't understand the underlying reasons a company hires one person over another.

There is only one reason that a company will hire a person (other than the owner's son-in-law). The company hires because they predict that the person they are hiring will earn their company more money than the company will pay out in salary, benefits, training, and payroll taxes. Understand this central concept.

A company will only hire you when they trust that you will bring in more money than you will cost the company.

You see, the organization you want to work for is not in business to give the unemployed a chance. Their mission is not to decrease the national unemployment rate. These companies are in business to return a profit to the owner and/or the shareholders.

So when my friends go to an interview with the sad tale of:

> "I really need this job. I've been unemployed for two years and I'm about to lose my house,"

The interviewer must, for the good of his company, his lenders, his shareholders, and his own family, turn down this man as having the wrong attitude for making money.

There are times of intense labor shortages, where the person above would be hired. Labor shortages like this happen about every 25 years or so. 2006-2007 was one of those times of full employment. I don't think you want to wait another twenty-five years to find a job. Therefore you must conform yourself into the type of person that a company will not only hire, but get in bidding wars with other companies for your services.

You Must Have a Job to Get a Job

The first thing you must do to get hired in any meaningful (read "well paid") job is to be employed when you go to the interview. In fact this will help you get an interview. An employed person is deemed more desirable and valuable than one who is unemployed.

This truth confuses many people.

"How can I have a job when I am looking for a job?"

You must take a lower paying position in order to be desirable to the interviewer. These types of jobs are available all over. Just look in the want ads. Your goal might not include selling paint at the mega-store, but it will put some money in your pocket, and more importantly, get you ready for a better job.

Too many people use poor math when they decide that since they make more money from unemployment benefits than from working, they should just stay home and wait for the check.

But these folks are not looking at the whole equation. A job, any job, boosts your self confidence. You gain experience. You meet people. And prospective employers are watching. Believe me.

Once, when I was between flying gigs, I took a job as the night manager of a convenience store. I worked from midnight to 8 am. My main duty was sweeping the parking lot and mopping the aisles. I was miserable and only earning minimum wage. But soon I got a phone call and I was off to Angola to fly for Chevron for a very nice salary.

A year later, I got an offer from a different company. The owner told me over the phone that when he heard through the grapevine that I had been working at a convenience store at night, he told his manager that I was a hard worker and that they ought to hire me. I didn't take that job, but that's a different story.

But you see the news got out that I wasn't just sitting around the house waiting for something to happen. I was out earning money. I wasn't afraid of work.

After seeing the poor performance I gave at interviews when I was unemployed, I never again went to a big meeting without being able to tell the hirer where I was currently working.

So, open your eyes for those jobs that no one else will take. I have worked as a temporary air conditioner installer, an armed guard, a convenience store clerk, and a truck broker. These small jobs lead to better jobs.

But my most powerful tactic was to:

Start Your Own Micro-Business

There is nothing quite so powerful in an interview than to tell the interviewer that you own your own business. You are instantly viewed in a different light. You are an owner. You are an executive. You are perceived as understanding all parts of the business: accounting, operations, and marketing.

Believe me, it makes you desirable.

In the first chapter I told you about the one man construction company I started. Over the years, I have also bought and sold airplanes, jet engines, aircraft parts, and diesel engines. When I tell my friends that they could do something similar and how it is like honey to prospective employers, they all say the same thing:

"Oh, I could never do something like that!"

We Americans have become passive risk avoiders. In our desire for security we have forgotten how humans live "in the wild." On my visit to Yellowstone this fall, there were strict regulations against feeding the wildlife. Park rangers know that if the bison and bear get used to free food, they would have a hard time when the tourists leave.

Humans are no different. You need to constantly exercise those self-sufficiency muscles that were given us by our ancestors. Even though your long term goal may be a job with Mega Corp, Inc., you need to be out in the economy making your own way. This will better prepare you for that job, and it will pay the rent and the grocery bills until Mega Corp calls.

How does one get out in the economy? Start your own Micro-Business.

I've had so many of my unemployed friends ask me, "What type of business should I start?" I don't know what would work for you. But I do know that humans are inventive. Sometimes it takes a shortfall of cash to awaken that creative gene.

Unemployed accountants can do the books for small businesses, unemployed writers can re-write company websites and sales brochures, and salesmen can sell.

One Christmas I was walking past a jewelry store, window shopping for a nice watch. The owner came out on the sidewalk to lure me in. We got to talking.

His business was slow. I was waiting on a call to go overseas, but I needed some spending money for Christmas. So I asked if I could print up some fliers and go door to door in the nearby neighborhoods to promote his business. We came up with a commission he would pay me, and all looked good.

I got the call to go fly overseas the next night before I could implement my plan. But there are thousands of businesses that could use a salesman who won't cost them anything but commissions.

So don't be afraid. Get out and start your own micro-business. Start a one person operation with little or no money invested. But you will have to invest lots of ingenuity and hard work.

An unemployed man came knocking on my door several years ago. He was dressed poorly, almost in rags. He told me that he was a recovering alcoholic and that he had just started a lawn mowing business.

"I would like to mow your yard, sir. I charge $15."

"Okay," I said.

"Do you have a lawn mower?" he asked. I was stunned.

"You don't have a mower?"

"No sir. I'll need to borrow yours." I laughed for a long time, pleased with this man's audacity.

"Yeah, it's in the back shed." Well, he mowed my lawn and did a good job. Then he asked if he could rent my mower for other jobs in the neighborhood. Each day, this guy went from door to door getting jobs, then came back to my house and pushed my mower to each different yard. He paid me five dollars per job.

In less than a month, the guy had paid me enough to buy myself a new mower, better than before. The man worked his way up to some nicer clothes and his own mower. I soon moved to another city and lost track of this man. But what a lesson he taught me!

If a recovering alcoholic dressed in rags and without a dime can start his own business, so can you. Use your imagination. Are you a good handyman? Do you know plumbing or wiring? Go out and sell your services. I've known ex-bankers who put together borrowers and lenders for a consulting fee. Others buy stuff at garage sales and resell it on e-bay.

I know one woman who was divorced and about to lose her home to foreclosure. For just a few dollars, she made a deal with a florist to buy all the flowers that were too old for him to sell retail. She arranged the flowers in small bouquets, and then went out and sold them on the street corner to men driving home from work.

"Take your wife some flowers. Surprise her tonight!" she would call out. In just a month she made enough to cover her back house payments. She had to stop for the winter, because it got too cold, but she says she'll be back.

Stop at almost any warehouse and offer to clean up and sweep, and some owner will jump at your offer. If you are mechanically inclined, go to any operator of machinery and offer to clean his machines and do preventive maintenance.

You have to get out of your house and look for work. Stop being passive, thinking that sending out resumes will get you a job. Reach down deep and reawaken those instincts that help us survive in the "wild".

Not only will you have money in your pocket, your confidence level will soar. You will be seen as much more desirable by the big companies, and since you now have executive experience as the owner, you can ask for a higher salary.

With the invention of Quick Books, you can keep good records. And be sure to fill out and pay your taxes with the help of Turbo Tax. They are both great products, and will keep you out of trouble with the government.

I can't emphasize enough the importance of current employment when you go into an interview. Being able to say that you work in the paint department at WalMart is much better than saying that you are currently collecting unemployment.

But telling your employer that you have your own business writing loan proposals and business plans for local companies (for example) is so powerful, so compelling to the hirer. He will see you as an instant asset to his company.

Seriously look into starting your own one man show. By doing so you can show your ability to plan, market, and execute your business goals.

Research the Company

In the first part of the book, we talked about setting goals. Toward the end of your list of goals should be the actual company where you want to work.

Learn everything you can about that company. Hang out with current employees. Talk with bankers and suppliers. Go to the library and research on the internet. You need to find out:

- What is the central business of this corporation? Do they make products like Caterpillar, or sell services like IBM?
- Is the firm profitable?
- What are their growth plans?
- How do they treat their employees?
- What products or services make the most profit?
- Do they sell internationally?
- What is the CEO like? The CFO? The Vice President for Operations? Find out the names and life stories of all the top management.

How does one go about finding out all of this stuff and even more? Sure, there will be annual reports and press releases on the internet, but how does one get the deeper knowledge in the list above? Yeah, read the industry magazines and scholarly papers, but they won't tell you the real, inside story.

You have to know and talk to people in the company. Let's say you don't know anyone who works there. Do some research and find out where these guys hang out. Does the company have a bowling team? Do the executives all go out to a certain piano bar to unwind on Friday nights?

You may have met some of the company executives when you joined the Rotary Club or the networking group. Perhaps someone in your network knows a person in your target company. Poll everyone in your network to see if they know anyone in the company. Then get an introduction and buy lunch for the friend of your contact. That person will lead to other people, and before you know it, you will be in their group.

Talk with those people. You may want to tell them of your plans; you may want to keep you plans quiet. My advice, I would keep your plans to yourself. Learn to elicit information. Elicitation is the art of gaining knowledge from another without asking questions.

Look up these two books on business elicitation. You will find them helpful. The first should be in some of the bigger libraries, the second is more of a specialty book.

Confidential: Business Secrets - Getting Theirs, Keeping Yours by John Nolan

The Dark Arts of Business: Elicitation by Wayne Taylor

Armed with these techniques, learn about your target company. You might find out that it is not such a great place to work, or that their profits are not as great as reported.

On the other hand, you may learn that the company you have targeted is about to jump into the lead with a new product, and you can catch the wave to the executive suite.

Whatever knowledge you gather should be reflected just enough during your interview to show the hirer your capability and knowledge. Powerful stuff.

Corporate Culture

Find out about the culture of the company. During one of my first job interviews out of technical school, I found out about corporate culture.

I had just earned my Airframe and Powerplant Mechanic's license which allowed me to legally turn wrenches on aircraft. I walked into a good sized air charter company and asked to speak with the President.

They showed me in and I told him I wanted a mechanic's position.

"You don't have the experience that we need, son," the white haired man said. "You seem like a nice young man, but we just can't use you." He started to hand my resume back to me, unread. At the last second, he spotted the final paragraph.

He took back my resume and read it carefully.

"So, you were in the 82nd Airborne? Light Weapons Infantry." He smiled at me. "I was in the 11th Airborne back in 1955. Infantry."

The man who would be my boss and mentor for the next ten years tossed my resume into his In Box.

"When can you start?"

You see, I had accidentally walked into an aviation company that had a culture of hiring ex-paratroopers as executives. After just a couple of months I was put on the fast track to management, and I became General Manager eight years later.

I was once offered a job with a charter company that specialized in flying touring rock and roll bands around the world. After talking with the chief pilot for only a few minutes, I knew that I was not going to fit. Drug use by the passengers was tolerated on the aircraft, and sex pervaded the flights and layovers. My short hair and military background were ridiculed even in the interview.

Another time, I worked at an aviation company where pilots, especially ex-military, were looked upon as a "necessary evil". This company was run by electrical engineers, and even though they had hundreds of pilots working there, none were in management. Believe me, it was a miserable place to work. I left after ten months.

So, find out the corporate culture. Is the company run by one extended family? Or is management all of one ethnicity or religion? You would not think these things happen in today's world but they are more common than you think.

Make it work for you. If you are Army, don't try to squeeze into a company that only hires Navy veterans. If you are an atheist and you find that a company is owned and managed by Mennonites, perhaps you ought to look elsewhere.

Corporate culture is important, and you aren't going to change it.

When you have thoroughly researched your target company or organization, and your desire is cemented to go to work for them, then you need to develop your Business Plan and then secure an interview.

Develop a Business Plan

The typical Business Plan is for an entire company or division. The plan lists the strengths of the company and how they will use those strengths to pursue opportunities and gain profit.

Instead of writing about an entire company, you will be writing a Business Plan about you! In it you'll highlight your strengths. You'll show how your strengths can be used, how much you will cost the company, and how much you will bring to the bottom line.

This plan is so powerful because not only does it show your ability to think, plan, and communicate, your plan will greatly decrease the hiring manager's risk level of hiring you. You have already shown him how you will fit in and how you will generate benefits to the company by increasing sales and/or decreasing risks and costs.

Decide how you will fit into this company. Spend some time thinking this one through. Just because you have always admired Mega Corp is not a motivation for the company to hire you.

You must monetize yourself.

By this I mean that you will assign a dollar figure to your plan telling the hirer how much the company will gain by signing you on.

Take all your good points, show your prospective employer how those strengths can be used, and then give him a reason to believe that he and his company will benefit from hiring you. After he reads your plan, he should see dollar signs ahead by hiring you. If the hirer can go to his boss and say, "We've got to hire this guy. He's worth $500,000 to us," then you have been successful.

"How Do I Write Such a Plan?"

Where can you fit in so that you will make a profit for the company? In Success Story Number Two, my friend went into a medium sized corporation and got a job based on his ability to get in to see the President and sell the Plan he had to make money for the corporation.

You too need to make a plan. I know that I am being redundant here, but so many of my friends try to vault their way into that great job with a simple resume and a smile. Don't think you can skip this step, it is the most powerful.

After you have researched the company, revisit the list of abilities that you put together in Chapter Four. Taking your notes from researching the company and re-reading your list of abilities, figure out what you can do for the target company to make them money.

For some of you, this will be easy. I am a pilot, so when I wanted to get on with an airline, I targeted the Chief Pilot, found out all I could about him, got my recommendations together, and went in for the interview.

For others of you, you will need a detailed plan of how you will make money for your prospective employer. Salesmen are always in demand, and can easily show how they would increase the company's sales and profits.

Plant managers, security specialists, accountants, and human resource managers will all have different presentations. If you are going for a slot as Vice President of Operations, your package will be much larger and more detailed than someone seeking a position in product design.

Put together a simple spreadsheet that will give a hirer an instant picture of what you will cost the company versus what you will bring the organization in earnings. Never underestimate the power of the written word. When you put your salary in print on the spreadsheet, that figure instantly becomes the starting point of the negotiations.

Warning: When you see and understand the amount of money that you could make, you might decide to become an independent business owner or a consultant.

Include a few letters of recommendation, a sample of your past work if applicable, and a single page biography.

Be sure that the whole thing is incased in a professional binder. Don't go overboard with a $300 leather portfolio and custom linen paper. But do make some effort to show your plan at its best.

Write your own plan. Paying a "hiring consultant" to put together your plan will only cost you lots of money. When you go into your interview, you must have passion, confidence, and intimate knowledge of your plan. That is the only way you will sell it and yourself as the implementer. If someone else writes it, you won't have that inner drive or enthusiasm. And heaven help you if your interviewer asks about some detail and you can't answer.

How long should it take to write your plan? Your timeline is different from everyone else's. I've written a couple of these plans, so I will be able to put together my plan faster than someone who has never written one. Don't worry if you take a couple of months. You now have an income since you are working or have started your own Micro-Business, right?

Chapter Nine: Getting the Interview

Many writers and job search experts offer the job seeker the same advice over and over.

- Find out who is hiring.
- Submit a great resume along with a killer cover letter.
- Follow up in a couple of weeks and ask for an interview.

This has never worked for me.

What has worked has been the uninvited interview with the hirer. Not the Human Resources gatekeeper, but the CEO, chief pilot, or the Director of Operations. Emphasis on "uninvited."

After we finish the interview, I have a resume to hand to the hirer.

For those of you who are unbelievers, I have done this for the last several jobs that I have gotten. As you know, my business is Private Military Contracting. The contracts change often. Some change every year. So, I have had to move from job to job more often than a normal worker. This is what I have learned.

Don't wait until you hear that a company is hiring. By the time that the word gets out or an ad is posted, the hiring decision has already been made. Often, the ad is posted just to fulfill legal responsibilities. Instead, find a growing company where you would like to work, and then go after the top guy in the department: The one who will make the final decision.

It is easier if you already know your business. If you are a geek, you must be able to make that computer sing. If you are an accountant, you count with the best. But if you are young or changing fields and lack experience, crank up the confidence and emphasize your personal references, loyalty, integrity, and trainability. However, even if you are the most experienced in the world, you will still need to make some preparations.

<u>Number One:</u> Be employed. Don't be needy for a job. It's a killer. Even if the boss never asks you about your employment status, your bearing and tone of voice will be screaming out: "I really need this job!"

We talked about this in the last section, but I must repeat it. Don't sit back and collect unemployment, thinking that you will get that big job soon. You must have some type of job or run a Micro-Business.

I have been a pilot since 1980, and many times I have been unemployed as a pilot. But I have always had a job when I have gone to a big interview. I have worked construction, mopped a convenience store, and walked the beat as an armed security guard. That way I had an income, even if it was meager. You must be able to hold your head up and truthfully tell the interviewer that you have to give your current employer notice before you can come to work. Many bosses use this as a test. If you will jilt your current employer, you might leave him in the lurch, too.

Number Two: Find a way to get to your target. Of course, one must first find this target. That means research, and it might involve travel. The first time that I used this strategy was 1987. I wanted to get a pilot slot with a specialty airline owned by the CIA. After repeatedly sending resumes, I called and asked to talk with the chief pilot. This is the conversation as best as I can remember:

"Yes, son, I've seen your resume and you don't have the experience we're looking for. You're too young. Call me back in a few years."

"Couldn't I come out there and talk with you?"

"No. I am really busy this week."

"Thank you, sir." I hung up and immediately called his secretary. (By the way, always be nice to secretaries and receptionists. Not only is it the right thing to do, but they can help you immensely.)

"Dawn. This is Dave Johnson again. The chief pilot said that he's too busy to see me this week. Can you schedule me in sometime the following week?"

"Yeah. How about next Tuesday at 10 o'clock?"

Eight days later I got on an airliner and flew halfway across the country. At 1000 I walked into the chief pilot's office.

"Hello sir. My name is Dave Johnson."

"What are you doing here?" the chief pilot said, recognizing my name.

"I have an appointment to see you at 1000. Check with your secretary."

"How did you do that?"

"When you said that you were busy all week, I asked Dawn to find a day that you weren't busy, and I came over to see you."

"Well, you have some gall." He checked with the secretary, and confirmed that I was scheduled for an hour. I got the interview. The end of the story is that I got the job.

In 2002, I called about a pilot job with the State Department. The HR department told me that I was to wait for them to call me back. Instead, I drove 600 miles to the secure military base where the Department of State Airwing was based. The guards wouldn't let me in, so I called from the gate to see if the chief pilot would see me. He did. I got an interview with him right then. I got another interview with his assistant the next day. After the final interview two weeks later, I got the job.

In 2005, I couldn't get to the Director of Operations for a company I wanted to work for. I knew him socially, but just barely. He was to meet with one of my friends at a local bar. As planned, I walked in about a half hour after they arrived, and my friend invited me over to their table.

The Director of Ops cringed knowing that I was going to ask him for a job. I wanted to in the worst way, but I knew that it was not the right time. I had one Diet Coke, talked about sports, and left. I never mentioned anything about work or getting a job. As I got up to leave, the Director of Operations pulled me close and invited me to come up to his office Monday morning. I got an interview. Then I got a second interview. Several months later, I got the job.

What is the point of these stories? Research the company. Go directly to the boss. Avoid HR until you are hired and you need to get an ID badge and fill out a W-4. Even when the company is not hiring, get in and get the interview. The boss might make a position for you. Or you will be the first in line when something opens up.

By doing so, you differentiate yourself to the boss. You prove that you are resourceful, that you really want the job, that you take initiative, and that you will solve problems. These attributes are highly prized by the big guys. Never give up.

Now What?

You have tracked down the Chief Hirer. By persistence and ingenuity you have gotten an interview. Now you are standing in front of his desk.

What do you do now? Be yourself.

You have worked for months to build up your inner person. Your character will shine forth. Lots of people pay for courses to know how to answer the 150 typical interview questions. **Worthless.**

A top executive will see right through that. Be yourself. You have become a hard worker, you have sought wisdom, you have gained knowledge of your industry. **You have prepared yourself.**

Your service work at the Rotary Club has given you the opportunity to contribute, speak, and work around executives. You network has already vouched for you with phone calls to the hiring manager and letters that you have attached to your resume.

You stand straight, unafraid, with your plan to help this company in your hand. You believe that you can contribute. You aren't asking for a job: You are showing the boss how much you can contribute to his team.

Your intangible assets will be in plain sight. Your network is evident in that you got into his office. Your plan screams out your ability to prepare and communicate.

Be yourself. You have worked for months to get to this point. All that preparation will come pouring out in your conversation, your enthusiasm, and your plan for the future. Talk half the time, listen half the time.

Be sure to smile. I know that this sounds stupid. Everyone knows they are supposed to smile. But you will be under some pressure. Some companies like Holiday Inn even count the number of smiles of an applicant during the interview.

By being yourself, you will inject a massive dosage of trust into your interviewer. His gut will be telling him to hire you, and his brain will be satisfied by looking over your Personal Business Plan.

There are different kinds of interviews. Some companies hire after only one thirty minute interview. Others have a series of three or more interviews stretching over a couple of weeks. I have been interviewed by one person and by committees.

The strangest interview I ever had was for a little company in Florida. They invited me to come for an interview on a Monday morning. They sent me a ticket to fly into Orlando Sunday night. One of the nice things about this company was that they were going to pay all my expenses plus $200 per day. So, I figured that at least I'd make $400 for going to the interview.

I went to the office on Monday morning, and was told the CEO couldn't see me in the morning. Several employees took turns showing me around the facility, taking me to lunch, and then dinner. All the time, telling me that the CEO was too busy. But since I was getting paid 200 dollar a day, I said, "What's one more day?"

On Tuesday, I ended up flying one of their planes on a maintenance test flight. I worked in the shop on Wednesday. I ran errands on Thursday, always waiting for my chance to meet with the big guy.

This pattern kept on going until Friday morning! I waited all week. I was upset because I hadn't brought enough clothes, I had to change my plans back in Texas, and I was mad at being ignored for a week. But I managed to keep smiling and thinking about the 200/day.

The interview with the CEO lasted less than fifteen minutes. Turns out I had been being interviewed all week by everyone from the other pilots to the receptionist. You see, every time one of them took me to lunch or dinner, or gave me a ride back to the company apartment, they were interviewing me.

"All my people think you will be a good fit here," the CEO said. "How much will it take to get you to come to work here?" We negotiated a salary, and I started the next week.

So be ready for the unconventional interview. More and more companies are using them. I have heard of applicants being taken to a team and asked to work with them for the day. Others take you around the factory and see if you really know their business. One of my friends went out on sales calls for his interview.

There are a couple of traps to avoid. Some interviews are conducted by a team. And it always seems to be one person on the hiring board who wants to embarrass the candidate and show him in a weak light. He is trying to get on the boss's good side by making someone else look bad. Be prepared for this guy!

The test will most likely come as the following question:

"What would you say is your greatest weakness?"

This is a TRAP. If you say that you have no weaknesses, the whole hiring board will know that is not the case and you will come off looking arrogant. Everyone has weaknesses. On the other hand, if you enumerate your weak points you look, well, weak.

This is where you pull out a success story of how you made a mistake and what you did to turn it around to a success. Conclude with what you learned along the way. This will make you seem even more qualified without sounding boastful.

EXAMPLE:

I once bought an old DC-7 airplane that came up at auction for unpaid airport parking fees. I ended up paying $9,500. For a 120 passenger, four engine airliner, I figured I couldn't go wrong.

Once I had possession of the maintenance log books, I found out the reason that the aircraft had not been flying. On the last inspection, massive corrosion was found on the inner wing spar. This old plane would never fly again.

After a few days of mourning, I got in touch with an operator who still used this type of aircraft and made a deal to sell him the engines for three thousand dollars each. But they had to come and take them off of the aircraft.

I contacted the local drag strip and sold them the 100 octane avgas in the tanks for 1,000 dollars. Now I was ahead by $3,500 dollars. I contacted a junk dealer who offered me $2,500 for the hulk that he would cut up and melt for the aluminum.

So, with a few phone calls, I turned a sure loss into a $6,000 profit for my boss. But the experience taught me to do my homework and talk to a subject matter expert before committing company money again.

You see how this story tells how I made a mistake. I leave it unsaid that I used poor judgment by failing to seek out an expert. Don't talk bad about yourself. Use the power of the story.

Always use a success story that has a happy ending. This showcases your ability to be creative and turn something bad into something good. At the end of the story, I delivered the moral, and what I learned from the experience.

Some variations on this TRAP question would be:

"If you are hired, what changes would you make here?"

"Why haven't you made more money in the past?"

"What was the biggest mistake of your current employer?

All of these questions are designed to get you to say something negative about yourself, about your past employer, or about the company that is interviewing you. Don't do it. Don't say anything negative.

If pressed for why you are leaving your old employer, don't tell the interviewer about safety violations, broken promises, or illegal activity, even if it is true. Just say:

"While I enjoyed working at XYZ Corporation, I am ready to move on to more responsibility and better compensation."

This will make you look classy. And believe me, the hiring manager will be thinking that if you won't betray insider dirt on your last company, he can trust you not to reveal the dirt on his company.

One question that is not a trap is the following.

"What would you say was your greatest business mistake?"

This question is a gauge of:

1) How much responsibility did you have?
2) How big was your budget?
3) How did you recover?
4) What did you learn?

Be ready with your best success story here. If the end of the story was not a happy ending, then have some very good lessons that you learned, and how you have changed for the better. For example, if your company went bankrupt, then you must have a good story detailing how you overcame and what you would do different the next time.

Practice your stories for these two questions.

The Three Most Powerful Words

Sometime during the interview, be sure to say the three most powerful words for getting hired. I would suggest close to the beginning, and then again during your conclusion, when you wrap up all the reasons why you are a superior candidate. Hiring managers all agree that today's applicant must be able to say these words, and perform.

What are these three words?

I can sell.

Everyone is required to sell these days, especially programmers and engineers. You see, technical people have access to decision makers. Plus, they carry extra weight when they sell due to their technical qualifications.

Receptionists need to be able to phone qualify and suggest products and services both to callers and visitors. Even the CEO must sell. Perhaps I should say, especially the CEO must sell.

Read some sales books. Sell yourself to the hiring manager first. Remember these magic words: **I can sell.**

Offer to Work for Free

You have offered your services and showed your plan, but the big boss is still not sold. Pull out this big gun only if everything else has failed. It may have taken you months to have gotten to this point: **The Interview.**

Don't let this opportunity pass.

If you are not offered the job right after the first couple of interviews, counter with an offer to work for his company for two weeks for a dollar. I used to offer to work for free, but the federal employment laws don't allow a company to do that anymore. Instead, have a consulting contract prepared showing that you will work for the company for two weeks as a paid consultant.

Price: "One Dollar and Other Valuable Considerations."

There are some types of positions where this plan will not work. In the flying business, an employer must spend several thousand dollars to train a pilot before they can put him on the line. As a private military contractor, a new hire must get a security clearance first. Another several thousand dollars. So for any business where your prospective employer must spend a lot of money to get you to work, an offer to work for free just won't fly.

This gambit works best for sales jobs, maintenance positions, management gigs, or creative stuff like web design, writing, warehouse reorganization, or business intelligence.

Use your imagination to reduce the risk for your prospective employer. My line is:

"I really want to work for this company. So I have an offer I'd like to make. I will work as a consultant for you. If at the end of two weeks I haven't made you more money than what my salary would have been, then you only owe me one dollar."

Then you pull out the consulting contract, all filled out. This is an impressive move. With a professional contract, plus your plan and your performance during the interview, you should be a shoe-in to a two week trial.

See the contract below.

CONSULTING AGREEMENT

AGREEMENT made this___ day of_____ , 20___ , by and between

___Your Name___, whose address is

_Your Address_____, hereinafter referred to as the "Consultant",

and

___Company Name___ whose principal place of business is located at

___Company Address_____ hereinafter referred to as "Company".

WHEREAS, the Company desires to engage the services of the Consultant to perform for the Company consulting services as an independent contractor and not as an employee; and

WHEREAS, Consultant desires to consult with the Company, and the administrative staff, and to undertake for the Company duties and functions as set out below;

NOW, THEREFORE, it is agreed as follows:

1. Term. The respective duties and obligations of the contracting parties shall be for a period of **two weeks** commencing on_____, 20___ , and may be terminated by either party giving one (1) days' written notice to the other party at the addresses stated above.

2. Consultations. Consultant shall be available to consult or perform duties such as set forth by the _____. Consultant shall not represent the Company, its Board of Directors, its officers or any other members of the Company in any transactions or communications nor shall Consultant make claim to do so.

3. Liability. With regard to the services to be performed by the Consultant pursuant to the terms of this agreement, the Consultant shall not be liable to the Company, or to anyone who may claim any right due to any relationship with the Corporation, for any acts or omissions in the performance of services on the part of the Consultant or on the part of the agents or employees of the Consultant, except when said acts or omissions of the Consultant are due to willful misconduct or gross negligence. The Company shall hold the Consultant free and harmless from any obligations, costs, claims, judgments, attorneys' fees, and attachments arising from or growing out of the services rendered to

the Company pursuant to the terms of this agreement or in any way connected with the rendering of services, except when the same shall arise due to the willful misconduct or gross negligence of the Consultant and the Consultant is adjudged to be guilty of willful misconduct or gross negligence by a court of competent jurisdiction.

4. Compensation. The Consultant shall receive "One Dollar and Other Valuable Considerations" from the Company for the performance of the services to rendered to the Company pursuant to the terms of the agreement. Company shall reimburse the Consultant per diem for any reasonable out of pocket expenses incurred by the Consultant pursuant to the terms of this agreement. The Consultant shall submit itemized statements of hours of services performed and expenses incurred during any particular month by the fifth (5th) day of the next succeeding month. The amount shall be paid to the Consultant by the fifteenth (15th) day of the latter month.

5. Employment. Should the quality of services of said Consultant lead to employment with the Company at the end of this consulting agreement, the Company agrees to reimburse Consultant for the two week term of this Consulting agreement at the same rate at which he is hired.

6. Arbitration. Any controversy or claim arising out of or relating to this contract, or the breach thereof, shall be settled by arbitration in accordance of the rules of the American Arbitration Association, and judgment upon the award rendered by the arbitrator(s) shall be entered in any court having jurisdiction thereof. For that purpose, the parties hereto consent to the jurisdiction and venue of an appropriate court located in _____ County, State of_____. In the event that litigation results from or arises out of this Agreement or the performance thereof, the parties agree to reimburse the prevailing party's reasonable attorney's fees, court costs, and all other expenses, whether or not taxable by the court as costs, in addition to any other relief to which the prevailing party may be entitled. In such event, no action shall be entertained by said court or any court of competent jurisdiction if filed more than one year subsequent to the date the cause(s) of action actually accrued regardless of whether damages were otherwise as of said time calculable.

IN WITNESS WHEREOF, the parties have hereunto executed this Agreement on the____ day of _____, 20___.

"Company" _____

"Consultant"_____

By: Witness _____

As the hirer reads your contract, you might get some questions.

"What do you mean by "One Dollar plus Other Valuable Considerations"?

Tell him that you will be asking for a letter of recommendation from both the hirer and from your immediate supervisor. If you have done an excellent job, you should ask both to write a letter. (Make it easy for them: Give them a letter to copy onto company letterhead. Let them know that this letter is for their convenience. They can alter it in any way or write an entirely different letter.)

These letters will make a valuable addition to any package you mail or deliver to a prospective employer.

You should also expect to gain some valuable experience and make some wonderful contacts and friends during your consulting contract. And in the "Work Experience" section of your resume, you will add that you have consulted at this corporation. And, of course, you will tell the hirer that you want him to consider you for the next open position in his company.

Buying a Business

This is perhaps the most audacious plan of all. But it works. I have seen it. You will no doubt be screaming at the page right now, saying:

"I don't have a job. I don't have any extra money. How in the world can I buy a business?"

I know about this segment of the business world because my maternal grandfather and my father's brother both sold their business for little or no money down. Also, I have had a man offer to sell me his property/casualty insurance agency with no money down.

Why would a business owner do that?

The business owners mentioned above were all getting toward retirement and no had one stepped up to buy their businesses. They each sold to managers who were experienced and the owners got paid off with part of the profits over the next several years. In some instances, the old owners retained the real estate and the new owner paid rent even after he completely paid off the business.

Right now, there are thousands of business owners wishing they could retire. But they have structured their business such that if they leave, the business will close. Each passing day, they become more desperate to get something for the forty plus years of work they have put into their company.

This can be a win-win situation. You, the job seeker, get hired immediately. Starting your first day, you get trained by the owner in every aspect of his business. Within a year you get a promotion and a raise. Within two to five years you are the owner for little or no money down.

Investigate this niche market by visiting around your town. You know from the opening chapters what type of work you would like to do. Look for a successful business run by a person who is getting a little older. These businesses are usually characterized by an owner who is the key worker in the business. Typically, these businesses have a steady and loyal customer base, a regular cashflow, little or no debt, and a proven business model.

What types of businesses are candidates for this strategy?

- Less than 25 employees
- Light manufacturing
- Service companies like air conditioning and plumbing
- Vehicle repair
- Jewelry shops and specialty stores

Research the business, talk to his employees and customers. After you have a good overview of his business, ask to have an appointment with the owner. At the appointment, tell him that you are interested in buying his business in a few years when he is ready to retire.

Just like your job interview, have a written plan of how you can help the business. Don't come in with wild schemes of national expansion; you'll spook the owner. Instead show him how your sales ability can grow his business by 20 per cent and how you can decrease his work week and give him the long vacations he's dreamed about.

But be sure that your plan shows how you will get more sales and profit to pay for your salary. In that plan, have it laid out that you will buy the business from him for no money down in four or five years. He may even wish to move out sooner.

He will ask for lots of money for his business. Of course, since he is providing the financing, he will deserve more than for a cash sale. But still, negotiate in a friendly manner. Set the price as soon as you can after you start working. Draw up a formal contract and use a lawyer familiar with selling businesses. If you wait to sign a formal contract and do well and grow his business, you could end up paying a much higher price since the profit of his business is now higher!

You will have to instill a huge amount of trust in the business owner. So, letters of recommendation, phone calls from persons in your network, and even working for free for the first couple of weeks will all go a long way toward making the sale.

Once you own the business, you can implement policies and programs that let you expand and even sell the business to a major corporation for millions. It happens all the time.

Conclusion

I know that you probably bought this book thinking that it could help you get a job by next week. It doesn't work that way.

But if you know where you want to go, you are ahead of 90 percent of the work force. If you make a formal plan, you are ahead of 99.5 percent of your competitors.

Follow your plan, keep track of your timeline. Develop your network and you will be able to get a meeting with whomever you desire.

Top positions are filled by top people. To get to those positions you must generate trust in the hirer. These top jobs are almost always filled by word of mouth.

Keep working. Keep interviewing. Your track record, your Character and your Intangible Assets are the reason you will be able to command a top salary. Bonuses are the result of your wisdom and work ethic.

One of the Realities of Life is that you must change your Inner Status before you can permanently change your Outer Status. And it takes work and a little time to change your Inner Status.

After you Become, then you can Possess.

Start back at the first chapter and implement the ideas and tactics set out in this book. Reread this book and do the exercises. Some sound hokey, some sound impossible. But they work.

The Great Majority get by with little jobs. If you want to have a good position, one that is different, then you must become a good person: A person who is different.

Those inner differences show themselves in the willingness to do what others won't:

- Work Hard
- Look at Long Term Cause and Effect
- See the Other Person's Point of View
- Think and Plan
- Persuade and Lead

Other differences will show themselves in the Assets you possess:

- Your extensive and powerful Network
- Your Training
- Your Education
- Your Health
- Your Creativity
- Your Ability to Communicate

Our young people are taught by the media and their peers that if you wear the right clothes and use the right deodorant and hair gel all the good things are going to happen for you. But these outer items will never put you next to the top hirers.

The truth is that top people are seeking out good people as friends, contacts, and business associates.

Become that good person, contribute first, work hard, and then you will be counted as one of the "lucky ones," and one of the "overnight successes."

PS: Reread this book and do the exercises.